THE BIBLE ACCORDING TO NOAH

Praise for Gary Kowalski's Other Books

SCIENCE AND THE SEARCH FOR GOD
"Kowalski has written the story of faith and science in a way that reads almost like a novel. It is written for lay people, but scientists and theologians will profit as well. The days of estrangement should end. No book has more promise than this one of hastening that end."—**John B. Cobb, Jr.,** *Professor Emeritus, Claremont School of Theology*

GREEN MOUNTAIN SPRING AND OTHER LEAPS OF FAITH
"Brief, wise thoughts from a fine naturalist and theologian who knows both humility before nature's grandeur and awe for human variety."—**Stephen Jay Gould**, *Professor of Paleontology and the History of Science, Harvard University*

THE SOULS OF ANIMALS
"Gary Kowalski's voice is one that empowers us to say in public what we have thought in private—that animals love their companions, know grief and joy, and play and create. They are truly our brothers and sisters in fur, feather and fin."—**Tom Regan**, *Professor of Ethics, North Carolina State University, author,* The Case for Animal Rights

GOODBYE FRIEND: HEALING WISDOM FOR ANYONE WHO HAS EVER LOST A PET
"This wonderful book is the best guide I know of that can help us deal with the death of our animal companions, whom the more we love the more we will grieve."—**Dr. Michael W. Fox**, *Vice President of the Humane Society of the United States, author,* The Boundless Circle

THE BIBLE ACCORDING TO NOAH
Theology as if Animals Mattered

Gary Kowalski

Lantern Books • New York
A Division of Booklight Inc.

2001
Lantern Books
One Union Square West, Suite 201
New York, NY 10003

Unless otherwise noted, all Biblical quotations are from the
New Revised Standard Version.

Printed in the United States of America

Library of Congress Cataloging-in-Publication Data

Kowalski, Gary A.
     The Bible according to Noah : theology as if animals mattered / Gary
Kowalski
      p. cm.
     Includes bibliographical references.
     ISBN 1-930051-32-8
     1. Animals in the Bible 2. Bible. O.T.—Criticism, interpretation, etc.
     3. Animals—Religious aspects—Christianity. I. Title.

BS1199.A57 K69 2001
220.8'59—dc21
                                                            2001029152

Contents

Prologue
Scriptures for all Species

T HIS IS A DIFFERENT KIND OF BIBLE, BUILT according to the same principles that Noah may have used in constructing the ark. Unlike that antique life raft, this book is not made of gopherwood. But my intent is, like his, to include every species. For sacred scriptures are like a boat—a vessel designed to carry a culture's accumulated wisdom across the sea of time, ferrying knowledge to coming generations of how we should live. And the knowledge we need most at this point in history is how to live in tune with the natural world, in harmony with the other creatures whose well-being is vital to our own survival.

The Bible is a very old document, which makes it extremely pertinent to those interested in preserving the planet. For over three thousand years, the myths and maxims within its pages have helped the Jews maintain a continuous cultural identity, despite

1

wars, pogroms, and persecution. And for fully two millennia, Christian civilization has been based on the unbroken transmission of holy writ. Admittedly, these are not the oldest spiritual traditions in the world. Aborigines in Australia can decipher the petroglyphs of their ancestors dating back forty thousand years. But any spiritual heritage that has managed to guide people and enabled them to endure over the course of many lifetimes deserves a large measure of respect. So many of our current problems stem from short range thinking. It would be foolhardy to simply discard teachings that have proven their viability over the long haul.

Yet part of what keeps the tradition alive is the ability to change and grow. Indeed, the Bible is not a single text, but a collection of writings that were compiled over a span of centuries, in dialogue with each other and with us. Interpretation is ongoing. Feminists have combed the scriptures to correct for bias against women. Liberation theologians have discovered the revolutionary message of the Exodus and learned to read the provocative parables of Jesus from the point of view of the poor and the oppressed. Such efforts can be applauded. But up until now, only a few have reviewed our sacred teachings to see what they say—or what might be criticized—from the animals' perspective.

That the Bible reflects the customs of a patriarchal culture is now well accepted, but that our religious traditions are anthropocentric—human-centered, as well as male-dominated— is not so widely recognized. But consider: although ours is only one of millions of species on the planet, few of the stories from either the Hebrew or Christian scriptures involve animals at all.

The relation between God and *Homo sapiens* is foremost, while other creatures are background figures, relegated to the periphery of the action. Think for a moment of the book of Job. We are told at the outset of the tale that the protagonist was a wealthy man:

> *There were born to him seven sons and three daughters. He had seven thousand sheep, three thousand camels, five hundred yoke of oxen, five hundred donkeys, and very many servants; so that this man was the greatest of all the people of the east.* (Job 1:2–3)

All of the supporting cast are killed rather unceremoniously in the very first chapter. The oxen and donkeys are carried away by marauders, the sheep and servants get burned up by celestial fire, the camels fall victim to Chaldeans, and the sons and daughters are all crushed when the house where they are feasting collapses under a desert storm. In the final chapter, however, Job's fortunes are reversed so that he has "twice as much as he had before," including fourteen thousand sheep and new sons and daughters. Justice, the reader is to presume, has been restored. But children and servants are only slightly more important than livestock in the context of this fable: fungible goods that function as mere possessions of the main character, who happens to be male.

Over time, individuals previously considered property—including women, minors, and those in bondage—came to be looked upon as persons, with legitimate rights and interests of their own. The Bible played a central if sometimes contentious role in that process—used to condemn slavery and to give it sanction, quoted with comparable fervor by advocates of equality and proponents of privilege. But for animals, the struggle to be treated with dignity has only just begun. Whether the scriptures can assist in that effort, or will merely serve to keep other creatures invisible and on the margins of our moral concern, remains to seen.

So many centuries of doctrine and so many follies and fallacies have been rationalized from the reading (or misreading) of the Bible—the subjugation of women, our sense of shame at our own bodies, the exploitation of the Earth. If only we could start afresh, with a narrative that could offer a New Beginning. In this book, I want to revisit a few of the more familiar stories from the Bible—Noah and the ark, Abraham and Isaac, Jonah, Job and others—to see if a more balanced and "sustainable" theology can be found, one where all creation is honored.

Some tales from our existing scriptures are patently cruel, as in the book of Judges. We're told that Samson, waging a guerilla insurgency against the invading Philistines, managed to capture three hundred foxes. Tying their tails together, he fastened a burning brand between each set of tails, then loosed the animals to run blazing through the enemy's cornfields. The author gives no hint of sympathy for the poor creatures. Samson is a hero to his people, and the book that lauds his exploits has scant concern for the four-legged members of the earth community.

Hints of a different attitude toward animals can be found throughout the Bible. The prophet Elijah is fed by ravens when he retreats to the wilderness. Balaam is saved when the donkey he is riding spies a sword-wielding angel astride their path; as the animal veers from danger, Balaam strikes the creature, who then speaks out in protest, finally awakening Balaam to the apparition that is before his eyes. Daniel is unscathed in the lion's den. Did the authors of such tales know that ravens actually do share their food in the wild? Were they aware that, whether or not they can actually see angels, animals can sometimes sense oncoming danger—from earthquakes to *grand mal* seizures—that people just can't detect? Would the author of Daniel have been surprised to learn of cases where people really have been rescued by the king of beasts?

In *My Soul Amongst Lions*, Gareth Patterson tells how he adopted three of the last "Born Free" lions: "Initially, I was their protector. Then came the day when they saved my life," fending off an attacking leopard. Other creatures feed us, teach us about unseen realities, and can inspire us with their loyalty and the fierceness of their love.

A new appreciation of animals is desperately needed at this moment. God's injunction in Genesis to "fill the earth and subdue it" seems to be the one divine commandment the human race has truly taken to heart. According to a year 2000 report by the Worldwatch Institute, eleven percent of all 8,615 known species of birds living on earth and thirty-four percent of all fish are now endangered. Twenty-five percent of all mammals are at risk. Will future generations ask why people permitted such a decimation of God's creation? The world has changed tremendously with the growth of population and technology and the problems we face in the new millennium are unprecedented. Meanwhile, the wisdom traditions and holy books we have inherited from the past have not evolved as quickly. Surely the myths and legends that have guided our culture and brought us to the present crisis could use a new twist . . . a change of plot . . . an environmentally friendly edition. The challenge is to reclaim what is healthy and revise what has become outdated and dysfunctional in our own spiritual inheritance.

What would our new Bible look like? What lessons would it impart? Would the snake still be the one who introduced evil to the world, or would animals become purveyors of grace instead of sin? Would a whale still swallow Jonah, or would these singers of the sea become agents of hope and redemption instead? In the congregation of which I am currently the minister, our children are invited as part of their "Bible Stories" curriculum to learn some of the more familiar tales from scripture. In their introduction to Genesis, fourth-graders are asked, "If you were God, what might you do differently when creating humankind?" My daughter's response was that she would give people tails and a good coat of fur, very sensibly observing that the appendages would be good for balance and staying warm. Really, who could argue? So much of our vaunted superiority is based on prejudice, inherited and passed along for hundreds of years until it has acquired the aura of revelation.

A new creation story should acknowledge that our species is not set apart from nature. Our humanity is inextricably intertwined with the existence of other creatures, and it's not so much eating of the fruit as imagining that we are separate from the Tree of Life that gets us into trouble. Like Adam, whose Hebrew name is derived from the root *adamah*, meaning "the dust of the ground," we need to understand that we are born of the earth and related to all earth's children not as masters but as siblings. Humility comes from *humus*: simple as the soil.

This book is called *The Bible According to Noah* because I want it to have room for the whole menagerie of creation. Mine is a biocentric Bible rather than a human-centered one. People are a part of the narrative, but other creatures are also important characters with major roles to play. And while I would not want to rewrite the entire Hebrew or Christian scriptures (there is so much good within those pages!) there are significant passages I'd like to change, beginning with the very beginning, as in this Jewish midrash:

> And God saw everything that He had made, and found it very good. And He said, This is a beautiful world that I have given you. Take good care of it. Do not ruin it. It is said: Before the world was created, the Holy One kept creating worlds and destroying them. Finally He created this one, and was satisfied. He said to Adam: This is the last world I shall make. I place it in your hands. Hold it in trust.

Those who treat the Bible as an inerrant document whose every word is sacrosanct may be scandalized by the idea that these old stories could be given a new rendition. But that is the nature of midrash; to adapt familiar story lines to changed circumstances or to dramatize new principles is a time-honored approach to scripture in itself.

Each chapter of *The Bible According to Noah* opens with a well known story from the Jewish and Christian canon and concludes with a revised version of that same tale—one that embraces the unity and diversity of life. My hope is that, when rightly understood and freshly interpreted, the Bible can awaken us to a new sense of appreciation for the gift (and the responsibility) that has been placed into our care.

Chapter One
A New Creation

In the beginning when God created the heavens and the earth,
the earth was a formless void and darkness covered the face of
the deep, while a wind from God swept over the face of the
waters. Then God said, "Let there be light"; and there was
light. And God saw that the light was good; and God separated
the light from the darkness. God called the light Day, and the
darkness he called Night. And there was evening and there was
morning, the first day. (Genesis 1:1–5)

LIGHT IS GOOD. WHETHER WE WALK ON TWO LEGS
or four, swim through the ocean or fly through the air, there
seems to be a consensus on this.

Near the slopes of Doi Angka, the highest peak in northern
Thailand, singing greets the rays of the rising sun. The chorus is
from a troop of gibbons, the smallest but among the most

numerous of the ape family who inhabit this region of dense forest and deep valleys. One of the first to study the habits of these creatures whose scientific name, *Hylobates*, means "tree travelers," was a Research Associate of the Peabody Museum at Harvard named Clarence Carpenter, who journeyed to what was then Siam with the Asiatic Primate Expedition (A.P.E.) in 1937.

We now know that gibbons are our fourth cousins—chimpanzees, gorillas and orangutans are all closer kin to humankind—but, at the time, biologists believed they might have been among our direct, evolutionary ancestors. Carpenter learned that these long-armed apes are experts at living in the trees, swinging Tarzan-style among the upper branches of the thick vegetation or walking two-legged along the larger limbs closer to the ground. The youngsters play tag, very much like their human counterparts, except for being airborne. Beyond the gibbons' acrobatics, Carpenter also found much else to admire: the apes' stable families, the monogamous loyalty they displayed toward their mates, the casual equality they seemed to practice between the sexes.

Any form of anthropomorphism (attributing human characteristics to animals) was considered scientifically suspect at that time. Hence Carpenter tried hard to remain the detached observer. But when he described how the animals greeted each other with warm hugs and little squeals of pleasure, he couldn't avoid the obvious: "The facial expression involves a muscular pattern which may best be described as being similar to the human smile." If the friendly and mostly peace-loving gibbons were indeed among our forbears, they were an exemplary prototype.

Carpenter also studied the animals' singing. East Asian poets had known about the gibbons' songs for thousands of years. Buddhists regarded the creatures as the reincarnation of human souls. Perhaps they heard a note of heartache in the songs, for those who had been disappointed in love, they believed, came back as these creatures who were known to wail to the moon. But Carpenter was the first to analyze their choruses with actual recordings, calling gibbons the "birds" of the primate world because of their complex duets, compositions that can last up to forty-five minutes, longer than the average Mozart symphony.

No one knows exactly why the apes sing, but observers agree on the musical quality of their calls, with tones so pure they seem free of the vibrato that accompanies so many human sopranos' voices. An article in *Science* describes the gibbons' singing as "a polyphonic *tour de force*." The female opens with "a brilliant theme lasting twenty seconds or more" that swells in volume from the soft opening notes until it achieves a climax of intensity and pitch. The male responds, beginning with a simple phrase, which he then embellishes and harmonizes with the repeated call of his partner, following an underlying score that varies by species but on which each singer improvises freely.

As in many species, the gibbons' vocalizations seem to be related to mating and maintaining territory. But Carpenter found an aesthetic dimension in the songs as well, particularly in the early dawn hours when the calls seemed to come from everywhere and the tree tops rang with symphonies. The cries were not mournful then. Indeed, the noise at that time of day was so joyful that the researcher concluded that something about the sun's first light "cheered the hearts of the gibbons."

Light is good. Notice that God didn't merely say it was so. It wasn't a divine announcement that made the sunlight more than okay and better-than-average. Rather, there was something about the light itself—its butterscotch texture, the way it seemed to dip everything it touched in honey, sticking to surfaces and making them shine that made the light irresistibly attractive the moment God saw it.

What is it about a sparkling object—a silver spoon, a watch face, a coin, or a bit of colored glass—that grabs the attention of a marauding crow? Charles Dickens, having acquired a new raven as a companion to replace the tame bird that had died some time previously, noted that "The first act of this Sage was to administer the effects of his predecessor, by disinterring all the halfpence he had buried in the garden." Why will a bower bird decorate its nest with a purloined collection of bright blue clothespins? The bower is not exactly a nest, but more of an elaborate museum, carefully constructed by the male, housing the most brilliant *objets d'art* that can be mustered: parrot feathers, flowers, aluminum foil, and similar bric-a-brac, sometimes stuccoed to the walls like mosaics, occasionally arranged within walls that have been painted (a wad of bark serves as brush, and dust-mixed-with-saliva as the pigment)—the whole oriented precisely against the transit of the sun. Highlights attract.

Light is good, although some do prefer the dark or what Genesis calls "the lesser light" that God created to rule over the night. Marine catfish are known to serenade each other with choruses that resemble the sound of a percolating coffee pot on summer evenings at the time of the new moon. Newly hatched sea turtles follow the moon's silvery beams which lead them from the

sandy nests where they were born down the beach and into the sea
(which is why beachfront development is so threatening to the
little Leatherbacks, who no longer know which light to follow).
And gibbons, also, are depicted in the antique art of China
reaching into iridescent, liquid pools, drawn by the shimmering
lunar reflection. God set both moon and sun into the dome of the
sky to separate the light from the darkness. And the catfish, the
turtles, and many others, liked the arrangement.

Don't roosters sing at dawn, and songbirds trill at the first hint
of rose in the east? Anyone who has ever taken a walk through the
fields on a crisp clear day has pretty much the same reaction.
That's how I usually start the morning. Going for a walk is actually
my dog's idea, and the path we trace is almost always the same:
into the park at the end of our street, then along a grassy trail
flanked by sumacs, occasionally looking across the lake toward the
hills of the Adirondacks before eventually looping back home.
Though the route is familiar, four-foot never seems to get tired of
it, and I don't think I could ever grow weary either. I like to watch
the sunlight catching the whitecaps, the purple shadows of clouds
moving across the mountain tops. I've even heard the loons, with
their almost human cries, near the lakeshore. What are the birds
communicating, do you suppose? What they seem to be saying, at
least to me, is that to understand Genesis we need to read it in the
present tense, not the past. The sunlight this morning is just as
fresh and unprecedented as on the first day it was made. It's an
achingly beautiful world, the Bible tells us, and we can trust our
instincts on this.

The Bible has often been called "the Good Book." The
section that Christians revere as the New Testament has

sometimes been called "the Good News." But what's so good
about it? What makes this old volume of myth and poetry worthy
of our time and consideration? The Bible is an enormous
storehouse of writings and, as such, it's bound to be full of
conflicting ideas and differing opinions. But if there is one
teaching that is primary to the Jewish and Christian scriptures,
important enough to give it priority right at the very beginning of
the book, it is that life is good. It's a wonderful creation.

God was so pleased with the creation of the first day, in fact,
that there was a quick executive decision to make some more. So,
according to the book of Genesis, there came to be dry land,
waters, and the firmament of heaven. Thus the stars and planets
and the seasons were created. On the fifth day, God said: "Let the
waters bring forth swarms of living creatures, and let the birds fly
above the earth across the dome of the sky." And on the sixth,
God said: "Let the earth bring forth living creatures of every kind:
cattle and creeping things and wild animals of the earth." And
God saw that it was good.

Isn't there a nature lover in all of us? Why else do so many
people watch public television specials or subscribe to *National
Geographic*? Did you know that a coyote will extinguish fires in the
wild? (Most other animals are deathly afraid of flames, but the
coyote is gifted with both the intelligence and the thick coat to
roll on a small fire and suffocate it before it spreads.) Were you
aware that Japanese macaques amuse themselves in wintertime by
rolling snowballs? (So far, these mischievous monkeys have never
been caught having a snowball fight.) And did you realize that red
squirrels tap maple trees to get the syrup? (As any Vermont farmer
knows, the sap needs to be boiled and the water evaporated to

make it palatable for pancakes, but the squirrel accomplishes the same feat by biting through the bark on a warm afternoon, then returning a day later when the oozing sap has been distilled and the sugar concentrated by the sun.) There is something fascinating in information of this kind. We human beings seem to be drawn toward the creatures of the wild like moths toward a flame . . . or crows toward a key chain.

I know I am. My daughter Holly and one of her young friends were hiking with me last fall on one of those brilliant October days in New England when the landscape seems more sharply etched than usual when we saw a garter snake, black and yellow-striped, hurrying across the leaf-strewn trail. With the help of a forked branch, I gently grabbed the reptile behind its head and lifted it to show the girls. Many people are afraid of snakes, and this may be one of the inborn fears we share with other apes. Clarence Carpenter, for instance, observed that gibbons are terribly frightened of pythons, their primary predator in the wild. Young apes in captivity who have never actually been preyed upon will exhibit much alarm in the presence of a large snake, while remaining relatively calm when around other, potentially intimidating creatures that pose no natural threat. Perhaps the role the serpent plays in the Garden of Eden is based on a long ago memory, from a time when snakes in trees were definitely to be avoided. If the two fifth-graders were afraid, however, they certainly didn't show it. Each handled the harmless creature and expressed surprise at how smooth and dry it seemed. We set the slithering serpent back on the ground where we found him, and he vanished in a flash; but he'd given us a memory that wouldn't soon be gone, recalling for me a similar encounter. A man was backpacking with his son when they chanced upon a six-foot rattler, sunning on the rocks. They stood stock still, hardly breathing, and carefully circled around the enormous viper before continuing on their way. "Dad," the young boy said to his father when they were in their sleeping bags some hours later: "This was the best day of my life!" The snake had given the child something that his life in the city wasn't able to offer—a sense of the world as it was originally created, before the Fall and beyond good and evil, nature undomesticated and untamed.

Perhaps this attraction to the natural world is something we've inherited from our own primate past. In the Kakombe valley, in Africa, there flows a mighty waterfall. The water has worn a deep cleft in the rock, plummeting eighty feet in a straight drop that sends geysers of mist into the air, showering the flowers and ferns that grow nearby with a delicate spray of droplets that catch and reflect the sun in ever changing patterns of wind, water and light. Chimpanzees can regularly be found by the falls, dancing in slow, rhythmic motion, throwing heavy rocks and branches into the pools (like kids who just want to make a splash!), and swinging far out over the stream on the overhanging vines. Jane Goodall, who has seen the chimps cavorting many times in their secluded forest retreat, says that the wet, remote beauty of the place fills her with feelings of awe: a sense that she is on holy ground. In her book *Reason for Hope*, she wonders if the chimpanzees also sense the magic and majesty of their surroundings and if their swaying to an unseen beat is inspired by the almost living rush of water and its mesmerizing, hypnotic quality, endlessly changing yet always the same.

We Great Apes like to dance. The German psychologist Wolfgang Kohler, who studied captive chimpanzees on Tenerife in the Canary Islands early in the last century, often saw the animals circle single-file around a central pole, wagging their heads and keeping time with an accented footstep to the rhythm of their own bodies in a primitive ring dance, often decorating themselves with garlands of rag or string or bits of vegetation to add to the drama of their choreography. Dian Fossey, known for her research on the mountain gorilla, once saw these wild creatures create a percussion ensemble, one clapping her hands and another slapping himself beneath his chin to produce a click-clacking of teeth as a third youngster turned "pirouettes" to the accompaniment. More recently, Adam Clark Arcadi, an anthropologist from Cornell University working in the Kibale National Park in Uganda found male chimpanzees thumping with their palms on the huge buttresses of the trees that grow there, producing satisfying, bass register booms with their hand-drumming. Each animal created individualized rhythms that could last anywhere from a few seconds to half a minute and be heard up to a mile away. Chimps at the nearby Tai National Park also drum, singing along with pant-hoots as well. Whether consciously or unconsciously, creatures like these seem to delight in their world. The earth revels in its own splendor.

As a clergyman, I know that a good many people spend their Sunday mornings worshiping G.O.D. (the Great Out Doors). Truthfully, who can blame them? For those of us who grew up as Christians or Jews, in a culture influenced by the Western religious tradition, the Bible has had a profound and lasting influence, shaping our values, affecting our attitudes, and molding our expectations about the world. But even for "people of the Book," the Bible is not the only source of our spirituality. The other is the book of Nature, the revelation of the great cosmos itself. The sky, the hills, the trees, the plants, and animals who seem so similar and yet so different from ourselves are perpetual sources of awe and amazement. Before there were any written scriptures, the earth was our teacher and soothsayer. For many of us, it remains so today.

My own heart soars in the outdoors. That's why the first chapter of Genesis is one of my favorite books of the Bible. Whoever wrote it had a simple, earthy spirituality. And in contrast to some other religions which tell us that the universe is *maya*—tricky, illusory, deceptive—Genesis tells us that the created world, in all its multitudinous diversity, is to be cherished and embraced...

We give thanks for the earth and its creatures,
And are grateful from A to Z:
For alligators, apricots, acorns and apple trees,
For bumblebees, blueberries, bananas and beagles,
Coconuts, crawdads, cornfields and coffee,
Daisies, elephants, and flying fish,
For groundhogs, glaciers, and grasslands,
Hippos and hazelnuts, icicles and iguanas,
For juniper, jackrabbits and junebugs,
Kohlrabi and kangaroos, lightning bugs and licorice,
For mountains, milkweed and mistletoe,
Narwhals and nasturtiums, otters and ocelots,
For peonies, persimmons and polar bears,

Quahogs and Queen Anne's Lace,
For raspberries and roses,
Salmon and sassafras, tornadoes and tulipwood,
Urchins and valleys and waterfalls,
For X (the unknown, the mystery of it all!)
In every yak and yam:
We are grateful, good Earth, not least of all
For zinnias, zucchini and zebras,
And for the alphabet of wonderful things
That are simple as ABC.

"The Alphabet of Gratitude" is my own creation, but the catalogue in Genesis is even more exhaustive, listing fruit trees of *every kind* on earth, plants yielding seed of *every kind, every* living creature that moves, *of every kind,* with which the water swarms, and *every* winged bird of *every* kind, the wild animals of the earth *of every kind.* "And God saw that it was good." There is nothing complicated about this kind of life-affirming, earth-centered spirituality. It requires no esoteric insights. A healthy animal can understand it.

The Almighty dotes on creatures of every kind. Asked what his long study of biology had taught him about the Creator, one famous entomologist replied that God must have loved beetles! His response was tongue-in-cheek, but still perfectly consistent with Genesis, pointing to the fact that with over 350,000 species identified (and perhaps several million still to be discovered), beetles are more numerous than any other beings on earth. Many are familiar, like fireflies and ladybugs (of which there are two thousand distinct varieties). Some are less well-known, but no less beguiling, like the wood-boring beetle the naturalist Henry David Thoreau writes about in the final chapter of *Walden*:

> *Everyone has heard the story which has gone the round of New England of a strong and beautiful bug which came out of the dry leaf of an old table of apple-tree wood, which had stood in a farmer's kitchen for sixty years, first in Connecticut, and afterward in Massachusetts,—from an egg deposited in the living tree many years earlier still, as it appeared by counting the annual layers beyond it; which was heard gnawing out for several weeks, hatched perchance by heat of an urn.*

For Thoreau, the insect's emergence after so many decades of lying dormant was a sign of the regenerative powers in nature, and in us: "Who does not feel his faith in a resurrection and immortality strengthened by hearing of this?" Resurrection is this creature's specialty. Beetles first appeared on earth about 250 million years ago. They were pollinators of some of the world's earliest flowers and remain the earth's "disposal crew," transforming dead and decaying matter into the stuff of fresh beginnings. When Mount St. Helens erupted in Washington, burying the surrounding foothills under boiling lava flows one hundred feet deep and obliterating all signs of life, beetles were the first to recolonize the burned-over landscape, riding in like hang gliders on the wind, their tiny corpses creating the detritus to nourish the plant life that followed. In their book *An Inordinate Fondness for Beetles*, Arthur Evans and Charles Bellamy observe that many of the scientists who study these remarkably diverse and imaginatively adapted insects "refer to their passion for beetles in terms of joy, excitement, wonder, delight, thrill, satisfaction, and fulfillment." To those with eyes to see, no aspect of the creation is too humble to elicit astonishment.

Life celebrates itself. But alongside this benign doctrine of life's goodness, there is another view articulated in the Bible. For after the plant and animal kingdoms have been created, God then says: "Let us make humankind in our image, according to our likeness; and let them have dominion over the fish of the sea, and over the birds of the air, and over the cattle, and over all the wild animals of the earth." Human beings alone resemble God, in short, and this resemblance sets them over and apart from all other creatures.

Little besides parochialism can support such a claim. As pre-scientific peoples once considered the earth to be at the center of God's starry handiwork, so they felt themselves to be the crown of all creation. Today we know better. Other animals dance and make music, love their mates and cherish their offspring, much like ourselves. They seem to experience life's spiritual dimensions as well, sharing in the qualities we usually suppose to be uniquely human. A friend who worked in Africa with endangered species showed me a photograph he had taken of a Mandrill, sitting quietly and gazing at a setting sun. The fading light apparently affected the baboon as it would you or me; the Mandrill stopped to muse, experiencing a moment of contemplation or enchantment. Because they seem so perfectly at home in their world, many animals might even be considered more "godlike" than ourselves: freer and less guarded and more centered in the moment. Nevertheless, the idea that *Homo sapiens* alone bears the *imago dei* would have far-reaching and destructive consequences, especially in the hands of the Greek philosophers who would shape Christian theology, replacing the earthy spirituality of Judaism with an outlook that despised the things of this world.

Plato began the process in his *Timaeus*. There, he explains that in the beginning the universe was twofold, divided between an invisible realm of thought and the visible world of matter. Between them was a demiurge, who first fashioned the primordial elements of wind, air, fire, and water, and then shaped these into a cosmos with the earth at the center, surrounded by rings of planetary spheres in ascending order. Next the demiurge made a world soul, infusing it into his creation as the animating principle of life and motion that sends the stars on their courses. Men also received a portion of this soul, although in weakened and diluted form. And man's task on earth was to subject the mundane sensations of the body to the higher promptings of the soul. If he succeeded, the soul would shed its corporeal envelope at the time of death and return to its more fitting home among the stars. Men who succumbed to sensuality during their lifespan on earth, however, would be reincarnated in their next existence as women. And women who surrendered to the appetites of the body would be reborn as "brutes." The process would continue, Plato believed, until the soul finally succeeded in mastering a body, at which time it would finally leave behind its material husk and assume a disembodied career in the sky.

Plato's pupil Aristotle (circa 384–322 BCE) refined this vision, distinguishing in his treatise *On the Soul* three grades of soul. To plants he assigned a "vegetative soul," which enables them to carry on the basic operations of nutrition, growth, and reproduction. Animals possess, in addition, a "sensitive soul" that animates their bodies and endows them with feeling. But according to Aristotle, only human beings have a soul that permits them to think and reason. Therefore, Aristotle states in *On the Forms of Animals*, "of all living beings with which we are acquainted, man alone partakes of the divine, or at any rate partakes of it in a fuller measure than the rest."

Christian thinkers adopted these conclusions. The fourth century theologian Augustine also distinguished "three grades of souls in universal nature," declaring in *On Christian Doctrine* that "a great thing truly is man, made after the image and similitude of God, not as respects the mortal body in which he is clothed, but as respects the rational soul by which he is exalted in honor above the beasts." Aquinas, the greatest doctor of the Church in medieval times, was able to discern five varieties of soul—vegetative, sensitive, appetitive, locomotive, and intellectual—but likewise agreed that:

> *Man is said to be after the image of God not as regards his body, but as regards that whereby he excels other animals.... Now man excels all animals by his reason and intelligence. Hence it is according to his intelligence and reason, which are incorporeal, that man is said to be according to the image of God.* (*Summa Theologica*, First Part, Question 3, Article I, "Whether God Is a Body")

Such distinctions are far removed from the spirit of Genesis, which states plainly that animals and humans alike were created as *nefesh chaya*, or "living beings." Yet Christian thinkers preferred Hellenistic subtlety to Hebraic straightforwardness. Later scholars, when drafting the King James Version, rendered *nefesh chaya* as a "living soul" when applied to Adam (Gen 2:7) but translated exactly the same phrase as "living creature" when applied to animals a few verses later (Genesis 2:19). The Hebrew word *v'yirdu*, which is usually given as "dominion" in English, was similarly misinterpreted. Dominion did imply "ruling over," but only as a wise king rules over and protects his subjects, or as God reigns over creation, sustaining, cherishing, and safeguarding every living thing. Scripture was certainly never intended as a license to clear-cut the forests, pollute the oceans, or drive other species to extinction. Nevertheless, the assumption of human superiority would become firmly entrenched and the Bible employed to assert our lordship over the creatures of the earth.

The doctrine that animals are inferior to humankind was never really a part of Eastern religion, perhaps because of the very different creation stories found in Asia. In the theology and philosophies of the West, the universe is "made," either as a monarch makes an edict, through divine pronouncement, or as a craftsman makes some useful object, for example as a potter shapes a pot. Both images can be found in Genesis, and Plato's demiurge as well as Aristotle's Unmoved Mover are also creators who stand separate, over and against their creations. In the East, on the other hand, the world comes into being more organically. The Tao (literally, "the Way") grows into the ten thousand things and every feature of the universe is a living expression of the Way. Whatever was most natural and spontaneous, least the product of artifice or contrivance, was to this way of thinking closest to the Source.

Under these circumstances, other creatures are often regarded as teachers and models suitable for human emulation. For instance, *Tai chi chuan*, the ancient discipline of meditation and self-defense, was supposedly invented by observing a snake and a crane in mortal combat. Its motions are patterned on the effortless fluidity of animals in their natural setting. Other animals were also highly esteemed. Gibbons, for example, were compared favorably with saints and sages for their good manners and serene disposition. In a Taoist text from the eighth century we read:

> These dark gibbons are raised in the lofty mountains of the south. Roaming about without a fixed place, they are always filled with joy and full of good cheer. When clouds and mists obscure the sky they are silent together, but as soon as wind and rain have passed they will vie with each other in calling. That sound purifies the thoughts of the mountain recluse, and it will move the traveler to tears. No stern punishments menace them, but they enjoy the friendliness of family relations. For their food they depend on what they find, and their bodies are protected by a natural cover. They are subject to neither taxes nor levies, they neither sweat nor toil.

"I am indeed aware of the fact that man is called the most important of all creatures," the author concludes: "But how could one ever gauge the universality of mysterious Nature?" Of course, the Chinese were familiar with the apes' music. When Li Yueh played his *ch'in*, a seven-stringed lute popular fifteen hundred years ago, his pet gibbon Shan-Kung accompanied him with singing. One official of the T'ang Dynasty observed that the gibbons' calls "have an eerie quality that penetrates your liver and spleen, and they reproduce the notes of our pentatonic scale." Because of their elusive habits, dwelling in the tops of trees and seldom seen at ground level, gibbons also became associated in popular culture with the realm of mystery and invisible powers. Many believed the animals possessed semi-magical properties, like skill in swordsmanship and the martial arts, or exceptional longevity due to their cultivation of *chi*, the subtle life force that was believed to circulate throughout the cosmos. But others admired the apes for more mundane reasons, like the degree of attachment they displayed toward their loved ones. According to one story:

> *When the lord Huan entered Shu, and had arrived with his fleet at the Three Gorges of the Yangtse River, one of his subaltern officers caught a young gibbon. Its mother followed the boat all along the bank, crying pitifully, and would not give up even after a hundred miles.*

Finally, the mother died of grief, throwing herself down into the boat from a high bank and perishing in the fall. Anecdotes of this kind generated a heightened level of empathy for the sufferings of these creatures, and while the practice of keeping young gibbons as pets was widespread, many came to regard it as cruel, partly because the preferred method of capturing an infant (then as now) was to shoot the mother in order to seize her offspring, but also because captivity seemed to maim their free-ranging spirits. A Buddhist monk reproached himself in this way when his pet ape's life came to a premature end:

You could be happy only when near your towering mountains,
You had been yearning for far plains and dense forests.
You must have suffered deeply being kept on leash or chain,
And that was why your allotted span of life was cut short.

This was at least one monk who found new meaning in his devotional recitations: "Sentient beings are numberless. I vow to liberate them all."

Animals also played an important role in the creation stories of many indigenous peoples. Among the Cherokee, it was an aquatic beetle who dove beneath the primordial seas that covered the planet to bring up the first muck and make solid ground where civilization could begin. The peoples of the Pacific Northwest regarded Raven as the creator of human beings, who emerged from a clamshell. For those of the American Southwest, the Coyote worked together with Raven to place two burning bundles of hay in the sky, which became the sun and moon, dispelling the darkness and bringing light.

The Creek say that the Creator made the animals, birds, and creeping things in the beginning, putting the world in perfect balance. But many moons passed and the animals called to their Maker: "We thank you for all that you have given us, for all the beauty that surrounds us. However, everything is so plentiful that we have nothing to do but wander here and there, with no purpose to our lives." That was when the Creator fashioned men and women, weak and helpless beings who needed wisdom and guidance in order to survive. And this gave the animals a reason for living: to care for these untutored humans, to teach them how to find food and shelter, and to show them the secrets of healing.

Animals can teach us once again the lesson we seem to have forgotten, that the earth does not belong to us, but we belong to the earth. And the creation myths of other cultures—of East Asia and native peoples—offer an important corrective to our own Western traditions, which have been shaped excessively by the otherworldly *mythos* of the Greeks. Such tales help us to remember that the sun was not given to nurture only one species, but meant to shine on all.

Perhaps the only way to save our world is by recognizing that this is not our world at all. Other living beings are not our property. The precept that we possess no title deed to the soil or air or water is prevalent among modern environmentalists, but this is also a rule articulated repeatedly in the Bible:

The earth is the Lord's and all that is in it. (Psalm 24:1)

All these things my hand has made, and so all these things are mine, says the Lord. (Isaiah 66:1)

For every wild animal of the forest is mine, the cattle on a thousand hills. I know all the birds of the air, and all that moves in the field is mine. (Psalm 50:10–11)

Indeed, the whole earth is mine . . . . (Exodus 19:5)

Scripture teaches clearly that the earth belongs to God. It is a goodly world, not ours to desecrate or despoil or grind up for profit, but a gift held in trust. Will we ever learn to behold the beauty of all creation and treat other beings with the respect they deserve?

If we do then, on that day, humankind will finally have seen the
light.

❧

*In the beginning, when God created the heavens and the earth,
the earth was without form and void and darkness covered the
face of the deep, and a mighty wind swept over the face of the
waters. Then God said, "Let there be light," and there was
light. And God called the light Day and the darkness Night.
And there was evening and there was morning, the first day.*

*And God said, "Let there be a dome in the midst of the
waters, and let it separate the waters from the waters." So God
made the dome and separated the waters that were under the
dome from the waters that were above the dome. And it was
so.*

*Days passed into years. And God said, "Let the waters
under the sky be gathered together into one place, and let the
dry land appear." God called the dry land Earth, and the
waters that were gathered together God called Seas.*

*Millennia came and went. And God said, "Let the waters
bring forth swarms of living creatures, and let birds fly above
the earth across the dome of the sky." So God created the great
whales and every living creatures that moves. And God blessed
them, saying "Be fruitful and multiply and fill the waters in the
seas, and let the birds and animals multiply on the earth."*

*And where the waters poured down from the dome of the
sky, like a waterfall from heaven, the chimpanzees danced.
And as the morning broke over the forest, filling the canopy
with soft green light, the gibbons sang with joy. For all*

creatures looked upon the work of God, and saw that it was good.

Then God said, "Let us make humankind, who shall be a mirror of my creation." And so God made human beings, female and male, and within their souls placed the light and the darkness, and within their veins God placed the seas, fashioning their bodies from the tissue of every living thing.

God blessed them, and said to them, "Love the earth and preserve it, for you are related to every living creature: the fish of the sea and the birds of the air and those that creep upon the ground and the wild animals of every kind." And it was so. Then God saw everything that had been made, and indeed, it was very good.

Thus the heavens and the earth were finished, and all their multitude. And on that day, God celebrated, saying to humankind, "Honor creation and keep it holy." And God rested, placing the world in our hands.

Chapter Two
The Difference the Dove Made

In the six hundredth year of Noah's life, in the second month, on the seventeenth day of the month, on that day all the fountains of the deep burst forth, and the windows of the heavens were opened. The rain fell on the earth forty days and forty nights. On the very same day Noah with his sons, Shem and Ham and Japheth, and Noah's wife and the three wives of his sons entered the ark, they and every wild animal of every kind, and all domestic animals of every kind, and every creeping thing that creeps on the earth, and every bird of every kind—every bird, every winged creature. They went into the ark with Noah, two and two of all flesh in which there was the breath of life. And those that entered, male and female of all flesh, went in as God had commanded him; and the Lord shut him in. (Genesis 7:11–16)

31

E VERYONE KNOWS THE STORY OF NOAH, OR thinks they know it. For many, the legend of the great flood is one of the first lessons they learn in Sunday School. For some it's a charming fairytale, for others a saga of survival despite adversity—a tale of traveling on perilous waters and arriving on *terra firma* at last. As science, it may have dubious value, for the Bible is not a textbook on geology. But in many respects, it is a beautiful story that deserves to be told and retold: a parable of caring for creation and of the power within a single individual to rescue and replenish the earth. Yet several years ago, I decided I was dissatisfied with the version that's found in the Bible. I felt it needed retelling.

My son must have been five or six years old when I thought the time had finally come to read him the story of Noah and the ark. As we sat down together on the sofa and opened up to the book of Genesis, I was looking forward to the experience. For my son is also a Noah, a name my wife and I had chosen with considerable care and that had special meaning for us.

Originally, he had been known as Kim Kyung Hoon–Kim the surname or family name that is common to about a third of those born in Korea and Kyung Hoon his given name meaning "meritorious star." We chose to keep Star, which seemed so bright and illustrious, as a middle name and reminder of his native land. But for a first name, my wife Dori and I wanted something that would express our hard-earned values—values that had grown partly out of the disappointments and dreams we had shared in our effort to start a family. Like many adoptive parents, we had been forced to wrestle with an unusual number of challenges to have a baby of our own.

We had postponed having children for health reasons. All through my twenties, I'd known my kidneys were failing—glomerular focal sclerosis the doctors called it—and I knew I needed to be physically capable before taking on the tasks and responsibilities of parenting. The same disease that destroyed my kidneys had killed my father when I was a small child, but I was luckier, living in an era of medical miracles. When I was thirty years old, I received an organ transplant that restored me to fitness. But ironically, the anti-rejection drugs that made new life possible for me had an unforseen side effect. Physicians informed me that the medicine had made me almost completely infertile.

Like many people, I had always assumed that I would have children one day. It was a shock, bewildering and disorienting, to find out I might never be a father. These were uncharted waters for me. For forty days it rained, in the antediluvian world of myth, and for what seemed an endless time I also drifted under dark clouds and stormy skies. Having cheated me out of having a dad, the universe now seemed ready to cheat me out of being one, too. I was inundated with questions. What was the use of living, I asked myself, if one day in the not-so-distant future I would die and leave no trace behind? Without children, it seemed, the evidence of my ever having existed would be washed away, as surely as if by some universal deluge.

When the ark was tempest-tossed and lost at sea, it was a dove who ultimately led Noah to safety, who told him the rains had passed and the sun had returned. For me, too, other living creatures were the guides who helped me to find the break in the clouds. Animals proved to be teachers and healers for me. They helped me find communion with a Life that was larger than myself. And although there were many creatures who helped me see the light, a single one—the dove—might be taken to represent them all.

What do we actually know about the famous dove that Noah carried aboard the ark? In all probability, the bird was tame. The wild rock dove of Eurasia was apparently one of the earliest animals to be domesticated. Some think its cultivation dates back to the stone age, and terra cotta figurines of pigeons have been unearthed in Iran that are over six thousand years old.

Noah may have been carrying the animal for navigational purposes, for very early on in history people recognized the pigeon's unusual ability to find its way over unfamiliar terrain. In ancient Greece, homing pigeons were used to carry news of the Olympic games to outlying cities and provinces. Julius Caesar employed the birds in his military campaigns to transport messages between field commanders and their distant troops. One version of the flood story says that after Noah released the dove from shipboard, the bird returned with red mud on its feet, proof that land had arisen from the receding waves. This (it is said) is why many pigeons have red feet to this day. Such an explanation is obviously fanciful. Yet it does seem plausible that mariners in Biblical times may have used doves to maintain communication with a distant shore. More than one ship in the last century, fog-bound and unsure of its position, was saved thanks to the quick work and keen sense of direction of a carrier pigeon, which can easily travel at speeds of fifty to sixty miles an hour across hundreds of miles of land or sea, day or night, with or without any distinguishing landmarks to guide it on its missions. No one knows precisely how the birds perform such remarkable feats.

Unable to explain it, scientists chalk up the pigeon's abilities to a homing "instinct." It might be fairer to admit that this is simply a form of intelligence that human beings can't presently understand. But in any case, it seems safe to say that the dove possessed an internal map far more accurate than any cartographers possessed in Noah's time. The bird was probably the best sailor on the boat.

On the other hand, Noah may have had the dove aboard for religious reasons, as a charm or token of God's blessing. In the ancient Middle East, the birds were regarded as sacred to Ishtar, the goddess of love and fertility. The Greeks, likewise, associated the pigeon with Aphrodite and the Romans with Venus. In what is undoubtedly the most erotic book in the Hebrew scriptures, the Song of Songs, the voice of the turtledove is a sign that the time for romance is nigh:

> *The flowers appear on the earth;*
> *the time of singing has come,*
> *and the voice of the turtledove*
> *is heard in our land . . .*
> *O my dove, in the clefts of the rock,*
> *in the covert of the cliff,*
> *let me see your face,*
> *let me hear your voice.*

For a man like Noah, intent on repopulating the earth, a pigeon would have been just the thing: a symbol of fecundity and procreation.

The dove's reputation is well-earned, for most observers agree they are endearing lovers, as well as models of fidelity and devotion. Like a few other species, the birds are monogamous and fiercely committed to their mates. The male typically advertises his availability with a deep bow toward the object of his affection. The female approaches timidly at first, but then more confidently as she warms to the posturing beau. Once a pair bond has formed, the two caress each other mutually, nibbling about the feathers of the neck and head—regions of the anatomy where self-preening is especially difficult. Soon the couple begins to play even more touching games, opening their beaks for deep kisses and murmuring sweet nothings in a display of affection so distinctive and so apparently similar to that of human lovebirds that the pigeons' behavior has entered into common parlance: "billing and cooing."

Except for being more gentle and refined, how is the courtship of a dove so different from its counterpart among *Homo sapiens?* Some might think it sentimental to ascribe such lofty feelings as love to a pair of nesting birds. But Konrad Lorenz, one of the original authorities on animal behavior, notes that love is widespread throughout the animal kingdom. Love, after all, is concerned less with reason than with emotion. And while the enlargement of the neocortex, the center of rational thought, is a fairly recent evolutionary phenomenon, the growth of the limbic system (the gray matter that surrounds the brain stem and that governs the emotions) began long ago. These regions of the brain are quite well-developed among birds, and most birds appear to have whatever neural equipment they need to experience infatuation, jealousy, and all the other pangs of the lovelorn. When one of the birds that Lorenz was studying lost its mate—its partner was eaten by a fox—the survivor showed all the signs of grief: listlessness, loss of appetite, drooping head, and downcast eyes. "In terms of emotions," says Lorenz, "animals are much more akin to us than is generally assumed." Calling the mating rituals of pigeons "love" is not a case of projecting human characteristics onto animals so much as recognizing animal characteristics in human beings. If only we could see it, love is all around us.

At least that's how it seemed to me when I was childless and forlorn. The more I learned about other creatures, the more I began to feel bonded to them. The world, which had felt so harsh and lonely at times, came to feel friendlier, more nurturing, as I gained a sense of kinship with other forms of life. When I discovered the care and attention that both male and female doves lavish on their young—taking turns sitting on the eggs, each sex feeding the chicks with a special "pigeon milk" produced by the same hormones that stimulate lactation in mammals—I recognized an impulse very like my own desire to rear and care for children. And the more I began to identify with other animals, the more adoption came to seem like a natural option. Pigeons, after all, will occasionally take in chicks that have no genetic relation to them, purely out of parental concern. A Mourning Dove was once observed brooding and feeding nestling White-winged Doves whose own father had unaccountably disappeared. Information like this had an effect on me. Where I had once felt alone, without any moorings, lost at sea, I began to feel related to all living beings, emotionally as well as biologically. I no longer had to grieve over my inability to start a family, for, I realized, if I would only open my eyes and heart, I would see I already had one. Our son's name reflected the belief that we are all related on this earth: Noah, caretaker of the animals.

When I sat down with my little boy to read the actual story from the book of Genesis, however, I was dismayed. I had identified with the life-giving themes in the Bible—the wet, windswept journey and the long-awaited landfall—but had forgotten the theological undercurrents that swirled submerged within the legend. For there are at least two stories here. While it's true that God is the first conservationist, careful to preserve a representative of every living creature, it is also clear that his attitude toward animals is ambivalent, if not downright hostile. For Yahweh (as the ancient Hebrews called their God) is pleased with the burnt sacrifice of animal flesh that Noah offers up in thanks for his deliverance, and says to his servant:

Be fruitful and multiply, and fill the earth. The fear and dread of you shall rest on every animal of the earth, and on every bird of the air, on everything that creeps on the ground, and on all the fish of the sea; into your hand they are delivered. (Genesis 9:1–2)

In the beginning, according to the Bible, all creatures including men and women were non-carnivorous. In the mythical realm of paradise, people lived in harmony with the animals. For in the first chapter of Genesis, we read:

God said, "See, I have given you every plant yielding seed that is upon the face of all the earth, and every tree with seed in its fruit; you shall have them for food. And to every beast of the earth, and to every bird of the air, and to everything that creeps

*on the earth, everything that has the breath of life, I have given
every green plant for food."* (Genesis 1:29–30)

But now God declares that animals are to be eaten and a great
divide opens between humans and animals. "Every creature that
lives and moves shall be food for you," God says to Noah. "I give
you them all, as once I gave you all green plants." (Genesis 9:3)

Animals, we are told, were originally created to be
"helpmates" to humankind. But upon their expulsion from Eden,
Adam and Eve are clad in the skins of other creatures. Eating
them appears to be the final step on the path from paradise to
perdition. Henceforth, animals are no longer seen as peers or
partners. Instead they have become appetizers and apparel—
resources, commodities, trade goods, to be used for human
purposes. God warns Noah: "Whoever sheds the blood of a
human, by a human shall that person's blood be shed." But for
other creatures, no such prohibition on killing applies. Ethics and
morality must govern our relations with others of our own species,
but are irrelevant as far as animals are concerned: "Into your hand
they are delivered."

But did people ever really subsist in oneness with nature, as
friends rather than as despoilers of the earth? While a place called
Eden probably never actually existed, the idea of the Garden is
more than make-believe, I think. People did, once upon a time,
live closer to the earth, with greater reverence for its inhabitants.

Memories of such a golden age can be found among many
cultures. In my son's native Korea, for instance, the legends say
that long ago, heaven and earth were one. Animals and humans
spoke a single language. And in those days, Hwanin, who

governed the lands from where the morning comes, sent his son Hwanung to found a new land in the east. There Hwanung ruled together with his three deputies, the sun, the wind, and the clouds, and they called the place where they lived Shinshi, which means "the divine city."

One day, a tiger and a bear who lived in a cavern nearby began to talk. "How happy and peaceful the people seem to be in Shinshi," the bear observed to her companion. "Do you think we could also become human and join them?" the tiger wondered. Together, the two animals went to petition Hwanung with their request.

Wanting to be helpful, Hwanung told them that while such a transformation was possible, it required much patience and long fasting. For wild creatures, the discipline was difficult. After many days of eating only garlic and spices, the tiger finally abandoned his quest. But the bear (who is considered the wisest and most enlightened of all the animals) persevered. And when a hundred days had passed, the bear's body began to change. The heavy claws became fine nails; silken hair replaced the shaggy coat. The bear had become a beautiful young woman. When Hwanung saw her, he was joyous, and called her Ung-yo, which means "the girl incarnated from a bear." Soon the two were married, and Ung-yo gave birth to a son named Tan-gun, which can mean both Lord of the Birch Trees and "Medicine Man." Tan-gun became the founder of Korea, whose people are descended (at least in myth) from the lineage of the god and the bear.

Tan-gun has much in common with Noah, his Biblical analogue. Both were long-lived; Noah reputedly expired at the age of 950, while Tan-gun ruled over his kingdom for 1211 years.

Tan-gun is credited with introducing the arts of civilization to Korea, from government to agriculture. Noah, likewise, is identified in the Bible as "a man of the soil, the first to plant a vineyard." Tan-gun founded a great nation, just as Noah's sons supposedly became the progenitors of Egypt, Canaan, and other lands. Even the intercourse between gods and mortals has its parallel in the Bible, for at the very outset of the flood narrative, in Genesis 6:4, we read that:

> *The Nephilim were on the earth in those days—and also afterward—when the sons of God went in to the daughters of humans, who bore children to them. These were the heroes that were of old, warriors of renown.*

Both Tan-gun and Noah are cultural heroes, larger-than-life figures that people around the world have used to explain their origins, folkways, and local customs. Anthropologists could quickly point to a dozen different far-flung peoples that revere ancestors who performed similar exploits and that share the belief in a "time before time" when humans and animals lived in such close communion that they could talk and even be transmuted, one with another. What accounts for the persistent myth among widely separated peoples and cultures of a lost paradise, a Dream Time (as the indigenous people of Australia call it), when humans and animals were in such intimate conversation?

Some feminist scholars posit that such a period pertained in the neolithic era, before people fully grasped the male role in sexual propagation. Fertility was a mystery then, and the earth herself worshiped as a goddess. The plants and animals, as well as

human beings (and especially women) were all her offspring. All
contained the same wonderful secret of birth and growth.

It was a lovely misunderstanding, based partly on confusion
over the precise requirements of conception—a confusion that
lingered well into historical times. The philosopher Aristotle, for
example, understood that male and female partners were needed
for procreation in most species, although he mistakenly believed
that the male contributes the vital "seed" to produce the fetus,
which is then merely nurtured in the "soil" of the menstrual
blood. But Aristotle was still under the impression that some birds
could be impregnated by the wind. How else could hens lay eggs,
even when they have never enjoyed the company of a cockerel?
Aristotle called such eggs "wind eggs," observing that "wind eggs
are called by some zephyr eggs, because at spring-time henbirds are
observed to inhale the breezes." Every gust of air, among ancient
peoples who shared such beliefs, must have seemed magical and
alive, charged with the animating principle of existence. Indeed,
the word for *spirit* was *wind* for both the Hebrews and the Greeks.

When men finally began to grasp their own part in
reproduction, however, a religious and social transformation took
place. Earth goddesses (female) were joined and often completely
replaced by sky gods (male). Nature was de-sacralized. Men gained
a heightened sense of mastery and control over the hitherto
unfathomable forces of life. They ceased to idolize the earth and
began to subdue it instead.

Admittedly, such theories are somewhat speculative. But it
may be more than coincidence that the author of Genesis
chapters six to nine seems so obsessed with the mechanics of sex.
Noah is told to take his wife aboard the ark; his three sons Shem,

Ham, and Japheth are likewise directed to take their wives (all of whom are unnamed). Repeatedly, Noah is instructed to bring two of every creature, male and female "the male and its mate." It is clearly a masculine, patriarchal God that is giving the orders here, one who is determined to assert the prime importance of the male in maintaining the race.

Did the ideology of dominating nature really arise when men became conscious of their own potency? Was the expulsion from the Garden an actual event ... not one that happened at any single time or in any one place, but a gradual devolution that unfolded as the forces of nature were demystified and brought under man's control? That would be hard to prove. But the idea makes a certain amount of sense to me on a personal, intuitive level. For in my case, it was a profound loss of control—the realization of my own infertility, my inability to reproduce—that brought about a complete reassessment of my relation to the world. It was painful to "lose my manhood" in this fashion, but the loss brought me an unexpected gain in empathy and admiration for the wild creatures of the earth. I ceased to think of life as belonging to me; I started instead to believe that I belonged to life. I began to learn that having a family is about sharing love, not sharing genes. And I realized that while the planet probably was not created for the express purpose of preserving and perpetuating me, I might have been put here to help preserve and perpetuate it.

For too many species, unfortunately, preservation is no longer an option. Probably no other creature has suffered more from human exploitation, or stands as a more poignant warning of ecological disaster, than our avian friend, the pigeon. Pigeon or dove, the names are used interchangeably by ornithologists for the roughly 300 species that belong to this highly social family of birds. Until a century ago, the most numerous of them all was the Passenger Pigeon, resembling the Mourning Dove, but larger and more richly colored. When our continent was first settled, it was the most common bird that could be found from Canada to the Gulf Coast, ranging from the Eastern seaboard to Montana and the west of Texas—more common than the robin, more so than the blackbird. Modern experts say that a third of all the birds in North America may have been Passenger Pigeons. Alexander Wilson, in 1808, made the first attempt to estimate its numbers, in a mile wide spring flight that passed above him in Kentucky for over four hours, stretching as far as his eyes could see in tiers so thick they darkened the sun. He likened the sound of one passing torrent of birds to the roar of a tornado. And indeed, roosting birds could weigh so heavily upon the branches of the trees that limbs up to two feet in diameter might be broken off, exactly as if a cyclone had passed. The naturalist John James Audubon estimated one flock at more than a billion birds.

But then the carnage began. In 1874, at a single nesting site in Wisconsin, hunters took 25,000 birds a day to be shipped as meat to grocers, blasting them from the skies and trapping them in nets. "Wagon loads of them are poured into market," said Wilson, "where they sell from fifty to twenty-five and even twelve cents per dozen; and Pigeons become the order of the day at dinner, breakfast and supper, until the very name becomes sickening." The slaughter was made easier by the birds' gregarious, altruistic nature; one bird in distress would give a call that would attract others to offer aid and assistance, all becoming easy prey for their human tormentors. The wanton cruelty of the hunt is a matter of record. According to one contemporary witness:

> As soon as it is ascertained in a town that the Pigeons are flying numerously in the neighborhood, the gunners arise en masse; the clap-nets are spread out on suitable situations, commonly on an open height, in an old buckwheat field; four or five live Pigeons, with their eyelids sewed up, are fastened on a movable stick—a small hut of branches is fitted up for the fowler at the distance of forty or fifty yards; by the pulling of a string, the stick on which the Pigeons rest is alternately elevated and depressed, which produces a fluttering of their wings similar to that of birds just alighting; this being perceived by the passing flocks, they descend with great rapidity, and finding corn, buckwheat, &c., strewed about, begin to feed, and are instantly, by the pulling of a cord, covered with the net.

The pigeons' decline was accelerated by loss of habitat, as forests were felled by settlers eager for homesteads across the middle West. By 1900, the last Passenger Pigeon living in the wild had been extinguished, the entire species gone. The dove, a symbol of peace, an animal associated with all that's tender, had entered into history as an emblem of bloodshed and of the short-sighted arrogance of human beings.

The assault on nature has gone too far. Maybe that is why I cannot believe in a God who would want to destroy life with flood or any other cataclysm; I have no interest in a *macho* deity who rules from on high. The greatest threats to our well-being today, in my opinion, come not from a celestial *pater familias*, but from the vaulting pride and folly of humankind—especially the male of the species. We suppose that only two-legged animals really matter and that we can bend the world to our will. From melting icecaps to holes in the ozone to the burning of rainforests, the results of such *hubris* are becoming increasingly plain.

The God who speaks to me is the one whose covenant is with all Creation, who calls us into wider and deeper relationship with the living community of which each one of us is a part. I find meaning in the promise God makes to Noah, as a guarantee that the world will still be here, not only for me but also for future generations:

> As long as the earth endures
> > seedtime and harvest, cold and heat,
> summer and winter, day and night,
> > shall not cease. (Genesis 8:22)

The greatest joy in my own life at this point is the satisfaction of having a family—a family richer and more varied than any I could have conceived a few short years ago. I am no longer quite so concerned about my own survival—given the assurance that whatever happens to me, life will go on. But that assurance has begun to turn to worry. What kind of world will my children inherit? How much more can the earth endure? If there is any way to save this fragile, blue-green ark, it will be by coming to recognize that we are not the captains of the boat, but rather fellow passengers with all that lives.

☙

When the world was very young, people talked with the animals. They understood the wailing of the wolves, the chanting of the whales, and the whistling of the marmots in the high mountains. All creatures spoke one language and shared the garden of the earth. There was peace and plenty in the land.

But as time passed, human beings forgot how to listen to their sisters and brothers who churned the oceans and leapt on the wind. Those who walked upright looked down on those who walked closer to the soil. People mined the earth to build fortresses and temples of brick and stone. They milled the endless tracts of timber to surround their towns with high walls to shut out the turning of the seasons. Human beings came to believe they alone possessed the knowledge of how to live. They no longer paid attention to the wisdom of the coyote, the fox, the wild geese or salmon.

Then the earth began to suffer. As the rivers were dammed and the swamps were drained to irrigate man's fields and bring water to his cities, droughts and floods began to trouble the land. Great storms gathered.

Only one man remembered how to talk to the animals, and his name was Noah. Old as the hills, he liked to walk softly through the forest, watchful as the deer. Noticing how each thing communicated with its kind, he listened to the notes in the branches overhead. But what he heard now disturbed him. There was a warning in the air.

A great flood was coming, the animals told him. It would rain for forty days and forty nights. The skies would open, the rivers would overflow their banks, and whole cities would be washed away. People and animals alike would lose their homes. There would be death and drowning everywhere.

Noah was afraid. What could be done to save the earth? He wanted to protect not only his family, but the other creatures who would be lost in the swirling water. An inspiration came to him. He would build a boat.

His neighbors thought he was foolish when they heard his plan. When Noah explained how the animals had warned him, they said he must be mad. But Noah collected the lumber he needed and shaped the keel for his ark, a vessel that would be large enough to hold two of every living creature, female and male, to save them from the flood.

And when the boat was finished, the rain began to fall. Small brooks became rushing streams, the streams were changed into mighty rivers, and the rivers outran their beds and swept over fields and valleys. Houses and barns disappeared beneath the surging waves. But Noah's ark floated above it all. Inside there were animals of every kind, from egrets to elephants.

For weeks they floated and for weeks it rained. And when the rain ended, there was no land to be seen. The flood had covered the entire earth.

Then, each day, Noah asked a dove to fly above the water to search for dry ground. And each day the dove returned without success. But the sun was warm and bright and the water slowly evaporated. One day, the bird returned to the ark with good red mud on its feet and a leaf in its beak, and Noah knew that land had again appeared. Plants had once more begun to grow. The next day when Noah released the dove, it flew away without returning.

Finally, the boat came to rest upon a mountain top. And when the water had disappeared from the highlands and the valleys were once again green with grass and fragrant with flowers, Noah opened the doors of the big boat and the animals departed. The kangaroos, the kingfishers, the koalas and the rest made new homes and began new families. And soon the earth was once more blessed with life of every kind.

As the last shimmering mists of rain were lifted up into the clouds, a rainbow could be seen in the heavens. It was a reminder of the beauty of creation. It was a symbol of the sacred circle of existence. It was a reminder that all creatures who live and breathe beneath the many-colored arch are holy and deserving of respect.

And when Noah died, his body returned to the mother that gave it birth, to rejoin the elements of earth and sky. His reason for being was completed. He was on the journey home.

So Noah's children and grandchildren told the story of how long ago the earth was saved and recorded it in their scriptures. And the animals, too, told the tale and passed it on to their offspring. But for the animals, the title of the story was not Noah and the ark, nor did they remember it as the Great Flood. The animals always knew the legend by another name: *The Difference the Dove Made*.

Chapter Three
Neither Victims Nor Perpetrators

*After these things God tested Abraham. He said to him,
"Abraham?" And he said, "Here I am." He said, "Take your
son, your only son Isaac, whom you love, and go to the land
of Moriah, and offer him there as a burnt offering on one of the
mountains that I shall show you." So Abraham rose early in
the morning, saddled his donkey, and took two of his young
men with him, and his son Isaac; he cut the wood for the burnt
offering, and set out and went to the place in the distance that
God had shown him. On the third day Abraham looked up and
saw the place far away. Then Abraham said to his young men,
"Stay here with the donkey; the boy and I will go over there;
we will worship, and then we will come back to you."
Abraham took the wood of the burnt offering and laid it on his
son Isaac, and he himself carried the fire and the knife. So the
two of them walked on together. Isaac said to his father*

Abraham, "Father!" And he said, "Here I am, my son." He said, "The fire and the wood are here, but where is the lamb for a burnt offering?" Abraham said, "God himself will provide the lamb for a burnt offering, my son." So the two of them walked on together. When they came to the place that God had shown him, Abraham built an altar there and laid the wood in order. He bound his son Isaac, and laid him on the altar, on top of the wood. Then Abraham reached out his hand and took the knife to kill his son. But the angel of the Lord called to him from heaven, and said, "Abraham, Abraham!" And he said, "Here I am." He said, "Do not lay your hand on the boy or do anything to him; for now I know that you fear God, since you have not withheld your son, your only son, from me." And Abraham looked up and saw a ram, caught in a thicket by its horns. Abraham went and took the ram and offered it up as a burnt offering instead of his son. (Genesis 22:1–13)

O NE OF THE BEST KNOWN STORIES OF THE Bible, and one of the most troubling for me, is the tale of Abraham and Isaac. The lesson I learned in Sunday School (the usual one) was that Abraham represented a model of faithful obedience. He followed God's will, and made himself subservient. But even as a young boy, or perhaps especially as a young boy who found it easier to identify with the terrified Isaac than with any of the other characters, I had questions. Why does God tell Abraham to murder his child? Why does Abraham listen to this dubious directive? Why does God change his mind? Why does he ask that an animal be killed instead of Isaac? And what manner of deity demands bloodshed in any form? The story is like a riddle. There is an absurd, almost incomprehensible quality to the tale. But it fascinates because it defies any simple explanation. If we had the answer to any of our questions about the story, we might understand more of the psychological and spiritual roots of violence. We might gain greater insight into how it is that men who consider themselves to be righteous and blameless in the eyes of God can take the blood of the innocent without any apparent feelings of remorse or compunction. We might have a window not merely into an ancient morality tale, but also into our own cultural narrative, which continues to create both perpetrators and victims with frightening regularity.

Cruelty runs deep in our society and in the hidden recesses of our private lives. As a child, sadism infected my own sports and pastimes and perhaps this is true for many boys. In the schoolyard, I watched playmates tear the hind legs off grasshoppers, then drop the twitching bodies onto a big red anthill. I also tortured insects with a macabre ingenuity I still find disturbing forty years later, trapping honeybees, which, once they were immobilized, cooked under the heat of a magnifying glass. I could fill a small chamber of horrors with confessions like that, but what would be the point? My friends and I, my cousins and the other children I knew were all killers, wanton and depraved at times, between our more innocent games of kickball and tag. And I wonder now how and why we became so cold-blooded. Were we taking revenge for feeling small and powerless, like Isaac, subject to the whims of a scary adult world? Were we inflicting payback for the violence we'd witnessed in our own short lives, mimicking the mayhem we saw on television and in the comic books we devoured? Studies have shown that children who have suffered a traumatic loss—the death of a parent, for instance—are more likely than others to engage in such bloodthirsty amusements. And maybe that explains in part why I sometimes mistreated other living things, as a means of venting pent-up anger. If I could not avoid pain, I could at least inflict it. If the universe could be mean, I could be meaner.

Don't we see the same syndrome among children who live in war zones, or high crime neighborhoods, or who come from abusive households? Because of their damaging early experiences, such youngsters learn not to trust others and to be guarded in their communication. Frequently, they retreat from the real world, which feels too threatening, into private fantasies, where they can feel strong and invincible, or into a world of alcohol and drugs where they may not feel anything at all.

The link between mistreating animals and other social pathologies is now clearly recognized—the American Psychiatric Association's *Diagnostic and Statistical Manual* lists them together under the single heading "Aggression toward People and Animals"—but the causes are still only poorly understood. Research shows that individuals who cared for pets as youngsters generally score higher as adults on psychological scales designed to measure empathy than those who lacked animal companions in their youth. And surveys of prison inmates incarcerated for violent offenses—murder, rape, assault—indicate that a high percentage had early histories of cruelty toward cats, dogs, and other unfortunate creatures. But many children will at one time or another act savagely and inexcusably toward a helpless animal, as my own experience suggests. Not all of them will grow into juvenile delinquents. The question is, why do some manage to develop internal restraints as they mature—conscience, consideration, compassion—while others seem to grow up totally lacking in these traits? There are no simple answers.

One man who studied the psychological origins of cruelty in a clinical context was Stanley Milgram, a professor at Yale University who carried out a series of famous experiments during the early 1960s. In a book called *Obedience and Authority*, Milgram described his operating procedure.

Two people come to a psychological laboratory to take part in a study of memory and learning. One of them is designated as a "teacher" and the other a "learner." The experimenter explains that the study is concerned with the effects of punishment on learning. The learner is conducted into a room, seated in a kind of miniature electric chair; his arms are strapped to prevent excessive movement, and an electrode is attached to his wrist. He is told that he is to learn a list of simple word pairs; whenever he makes an error, he will receive electric shocks of increasing intensity.

He needn't worry about it much, since the shocks aren't real. The man in the electric chair is just an actor. But the other participant, who is the actual focus of the experiment, doesn't know that. After watching the learner being strapped into place, he is seated in front of an impressive shock generator, with an instrument panel of thirty lever switches labeled with voltage designations of increasing intensity, from 15 to 450 volts. The point of the experiment is to see how far a person will go along with orders to inflict pain on an unwilling victim.

As the shocks move up the scale, so do the learner's outcries. At 75 volts, he grunts; at 120 volts, he complains loudly; at 150, he demands to be released from the experiment. As the voltage increases, his protests become more vehement and emotional, until he begins screaming, and at the highest levels makes no sound at all.

For the teacher, Milgram comments, the situation quickly becomes one of gripping tension.

> *It is not a game for him; conflict is intense and obvious. The manifest suffering of the learner presses him to quit; but each time he hesitates to administer a shock, the experimenter orders him to continue. To extricate himself from this plight, the subject must make a clear break with authority.*

The analogy to the story of Abraham and Isaac should be evident. Like the subjects in Milgram's experiment, Abraham is caught in a moral dilemma. Commanded to kill his own son, he must make a choice: follow directions and carry out an act of wanton destruction or resist orders. Abraham's response, as it turns out, was not so unusual. Most people do as they are told.

Before carrying out the experiment, Milgram asked various people to predict how subjects would react to their ethical predicament. Almost all of those surveyed forecast that compliance would be minimal. Experts and laypeople alike assumed that when told to deliver the shocks, the "teacher" would back out or call the bluff. The actual results of the experiment showed the opposite. The large majority of the subjects obeyed the experimenter to the very end, punishing the victim until they reached the most potent shock available on the generator. Like

Abraham, they were prepared to go to the limit rather than question what they understood to be the rules.

The experiment has disturbing implications. It leads to the conclusion that most people are capable of torturing and systematically abusing others under the right circumstances. The voice of conscience, along with the moral precepts we have heard since childhood (expressed in Judaism as "love to God and neighbor," and in Christianity as "Do unto others as you would have others do unto you," a golden rule common to all religions) appear weak and uncertain guides when confronted by a man in a lab coat or another authority figure who demands that we inflict pain and injury on those who are helpless to resist.

Another experiment that parallels Milgram's research raises similar concerns. It was carried out at about the same time, and reported in the *American Journal of Psychiatry* in 1964.

In this experiment, rhesus monkeys, also known as macaques, were confined in a laboratory where they were trained to receive food by pulling on one of two chains, right or left, depending on the color of a flashing light. After they had properly learned the sequence, another monkey was introduced, visible through a one-way mirror and held in restraints. By pulling the chains in the correct fashion, the first monkey could still get his snack, but one of the chains now delivered a powerful electric shock to the other animal whose agony was in plain view. In effect, animals who refused to deliver the shock were cut to starvation rations. Trapped in this situation, it was discovered that most of the monkeys would not cooperate. In one experiment, only thirteen percent would deliver the shock—eighty-seven percent chose to go hungry instead. One of the animals refused to pull either of the chains and went without food for twelve days rather than hurt its companion. The experimenters, who were interested in learning whether kinship plays a role in altruistic behavior, found that unrelated macaques were just as likely to be spared as those who were genetically similar. Only one variable really seemed to predict how the animal would respond to the dilemma. Monkeys who had been shocked in previous experiments themselves were even less willing to pull the chain and subject others to such torment.

In their book *Shadows of Forgotten Ancestors* where they describe this research, Carl Sagan and Ann Druyan ask what kind of scientists devise such nightmarish scenarios, noting that their own sympathies lie with the lab animals—preferring to suffer real agony themselves before inflicting pain on another—rather than with the technicians who subjected them to such treatment.

> *But their experiments permit us to glimpse in non-humans a saintly willingness to make sacrifices in order to save others— even those who are not close kin. By conventional human standards, these macaques, who have never gone to Sunday School, never heard of the Ten Commandments, never squirmed through a single junior high civics lesson—seem exemplary in their moral grounding and their courageous resistance to evil.*

This experiment also poses provocative questions. I wonder, for instance, whether the individuals implicated in Milgram's study would have been so willing to obey the man in the white coat if they had previously given more thought to the ethics of applying electric shocks to any living creature, be it a person or some other primate. Would a convinced anti-vivisectionist, one who opposes the use of animals in laboratories in general, have been as willing to steadily increase the voltage on command when human subjects were involved? Possibly, though it seems fairly unlikely. Most of those in Milgram's study appeared to struggle inwardly with the ethical tension between their natural reluctance to harm another person and their desire to please and placate the man in charge. Perhaps they were able to overcome their initial reluctance to inflict pain on another because they were able to place their actions, consciously or unconsciously, within another moral framework—the framework of the animal laboratory, where the gathering of data is considered paramount and the cost in pain and suffering counts for little or nothing.

That hypothesis would be consistent with the work of Charles Sheridan and Richard King, two would-be followers of Stanley Milgram who decided to carry his research one step further by administering real shocks instead of phoney ones. As they describe it in an article that appeared in the *Proceedings of the American Psychological Association* in 1972:

> *In this experiment the learner-victim was actually given shocks. A nonhuman subject—a cute, fluffy puppy—was substituted for the human learner-victim of Milgram's paradigm. In addition, shocks were amperage-limited and capable of creating responses such as running, howling, and yelping [which the researchers assure readers did not actually hurt the dog] ... The first of the three actual voltage levels produced foot flexion and occasional barks, the second level produced running and*

*vocalization, and the final level resulted in continuous barking
and howling.*

As in the original research, most of the human subjects (college
students in this case) experienced acute distress in this morally
compromised setting. Although they had been told that the
puppy was being trained to discriminate between flickering and
steady lights, the experiment was in fact designed to give the dog
a painful jolt no matter how he responded to the stimulus. Both
the animal and the trainer were unknowingly caught in an
insoluble predicament. Many tried to gently coax the puppy to
escape the shock, to no avail; others shifted nervously from foot
to foot, as if sympathizing with the animal whose paws were
trapped on the electric grid. Some hyperventilated, gasping for air,
or even began to cry. As in Milgram's experiments, however, those
who protested were sternly reminded that they had no choice and
must continue with the regimen of punishment. Having been
informed at the outset that this was an "important" scientific
investigation into the "critical fusion frequency" in canine vision,
almost all suppressed their own better instincts and ultimately
surrendered to authority.

It is seemingly a small step from shocking puppies (regarded as
standard practice in animal research, where much worse things
are routine) to giving real shocks to real people (still looked upon
as off limits by most ethicists). This leads to the next point. For
what I want to suggest is that just as Abraham was able to
substitute a human for an animal sacrifice—and expressed an
equal willingness to take the life of a kid, be it two-legged or four-
legged—people living in our own time may make similar

substitutions. Of course, we no longer inhabit a world in which ritual slayings are a part of our ordinary experience. The thought of ceremonially killing an animal as an act of divine worship is abhorrent for most of us. Still, we can understand that in Abraham's time, some four thousand years ago, such practices were commonplace—so common, indeed, that human sacrifice was an accepted element of many cultures.

The story of Abraham, or Abram, as he is also called, follows shortly after that of Noah. Noah's saga ends in the ninth chapter of Genesis; Abraham's begins in chapter eleven, but in that short space we move from the timeless realm of myth into the world of semi-historical characters and events. We learn that Abraham's family originated in the city of Ur, in southern Mesopotamia. He was called by God out of that land, traveling up the rich Tigris–Euphrates valley to Haran, a flourishing center in Anatolia. After a sojourn in Egypt, Abraham finally settled in Palestine, the land promised to him by God, where he would spend the remainder of his life. But before his death, he would send his servant back to the land of his birth, to Mesopotamia, to find a wife for his son Isaac.

With this cultural background, Abraham would have been well acquainted with human as well as animal sacrifices. Mesopotamian texts of the first millennium BCE speak of the cremation of male children in honor of the god Hadad. Several references in Hebrew scriptures also refer to the passing of children through fire to Molech, a Mesopotamian deity known to have been worshiped in Ur during the time that Abraham must have lived. Phoenicians (who were culturally and linguistically closely related to their Israelite neighbors) were particularly notorious for the practice. Such burnt offerings might have many purposes—to appease a deity or render thanks, to fulfill a vow or pay a pledge—and were surrounded with complex ritual laws defining acceptable victims, who were usually young. Immolation was the most common form of death. Though we cannot know exactly what human blood offerings entailed, the furious denunciations in Deuteronomy of "those who burn their sons and their daughters in the fire to the gods," accompanied by stern warning to the Israelites not to engage in such abominations, suggest that the custom not only existed among Israel's ancient Near Eastern neighbors, but that the descendants of Abraham needed strong admonitions not to engage in the practice themselves.

Human and animal sacrifice thus reinforced and complemented one another; they were close cousins within an archaic world view. And there is at least textual evidence that human sacrifice was practiced in ancient Israel. The book of Exodus commands, "The firstborn of your sons you shall give to me. You shall do the same with your oxen and with your sheep" (Exodus 22:29), while the prophet Jeremiah complains that the people of Judah "burn their sons and their daughters in the fire" (Jeremiah 7:31). The binding of Isaac has been interpreted by some scholars as a polemic against the child sacrifice that was pervasive in the ancient Near East. But Abraham's apparent willingness to murder his own son—and the praise bestowed for his readiness to surrender his firstborn—reflects a more complicated picture. Very probably human sacrifice not only occurred but was even sanctioned among the tribal ancestors of the Hebrew people, with children only gradually giving way to

animals as sacrificial victims. Later prophets like Isaiah would
attack all forms of living sacrifice: "Whoever slaughters an ox is
like one who kills a human being" (Isaiah 66:3). Perhaps Isaiah,
Amos, and similar reformers, who called for a religion rooted in
justice and mercy rather than one based on burnt offerings,
realized that so long as animal sacrifice remained a feature of the
religious landscape, human sacrifice remained a persistent
possibility. There was always the danger of backsliding. So long as
the ritual machinery remained in place, the victims might be
interchangeable.

The machinery of the laboratory, I want to suggest, plays a
comparable role in modern society. Like the primitive machinery
of sacrifice, it has its own mystique, its own priesthood, its own
structures of plausibility. It generates a mental and moral universe
that operates by its own distinct rules. Within that universe, for
instance, duplicity is an accepted norm. Shocking puppies can be
represented as an "important" inquiry on visual perception, when
in fact it is merely a study in how easily people can be bullied into
submission. Within that moral universe, almost anything goes.
But once the framework has been established, it must be
maintained. It enforces its own imperatives. The issue of who gets
hurt then becomes subordinate to the smooth functioning of the
apparatus.

The boundary separating human and non-human is easily
blurred in such situations, as it was in Nazi Germany, where Jews,
gypsies, homosexuals, and many others became guinea pigs for
various forms of medical experimentation. One woman who
survived the notorious Block 10 in Auschwitz recalled being
"locked up as animals in a cage." Another imprisoned in the same

camp observed that for the Nazis, "man was the cheapest experimental animal ... cheaper than a rat," while survivors who encountered the notorious camp physician Josef Mengele testified that he treated the prisoners like mice. In the Ravensbruck concentration camp, bone transplants and other experiments were conducted on women who were actually nicknamed "rabbits." This identification of human with animal was an explicit element in the pseudo-science of Nazism. Ernst Haeckel, a biologist who became a chief propagandist for Nazi ideology asserted bluntly that since the so-called "lower races" are "psychologically nearer to the mammals (apes and dogs) than to civilized Europeans, we must therefore, assign a totally different value to their lives."

Traditionally, of course, animals have been considered to have no intrinsic value in Western culture. Philosophers from Thomas Aquinas to Immanuel Kant have affirmed that we have no ethical duties except toward our own species. Animals may have value insofar as they can be used as research tools or for other human purposes, but they have no worth in and of themselves. According to this reasoning, non-humans stand outside the realm of rights and responsibilities that define our moral order. But when a broad category of beings exists whose lives are considered expendable, almost anyone can be assigned there, and once they have been reclassified as less than fully human, they too can be exploited and manipulated with impunity. Since many of the SS officers who ran the laboratories had long experience with pharmaceutical firms and other research establishments, it presumably required only a small psychological transition to enable them to apply to

Jews the same principle they had applied to other sub-species: "Everything is permitted."

Holocaust was a term first used to describe the fiery consummation of animals upon the altar in ancient Israel. In our time the word *holocaust* has taken on a terrible new meaning. But the ancient and modern usages are not entirely unrelated. Nobel prize winning author Isaac Bashevis Singer wrote, "As long as human beings go on shedding the blood of animals, there will never be any peace." As a Jewish survivor of Nazi-dominated Europe, Singer spoke with firsthand authority. Born the son of a poor rabbi in a small Polish village, he narrowly escaped death himself, emigrating to the United States in 1935. The author's mother and brother perished four years later in the general extermination. Singer saw how brutality begins, and how it spreads:

> *There is only one little step from killing animals to creating gas chambers á la Hitler and concentration camps á la Stalin. There will be no justice as long as man will stand with a knife or a gun and destroy those who are weaker than he is.*

As Singer predicted, the abuse of animals opened the door to other forms of violence.

In many cases, animal testing appears to have paved the way for human experimentation. The Third Reich's greatest authority on gas warfare, for instance, was Otto Bickenbach, on the medical faculty of the University of Strasbourg. He had conducted extensive animal experiments with phosgene, a vapor that sears lung tissue on contact, and developed the drug utropine to treat the burns. In 1943, Bickenbach was persuaded to use prisoners in the Natzweiler concentration camp to further study the effects of the deadly gas—continuing his earlier line of research, but substituting human for non-human subjects. After the war, he was sentenced to twenty years hard labor by the Nuremberg Tribunal. Doctor Eugen Haagen was another pre-eminent medical practitioner whose extensive studies on animal immunology helped to produce a vaccine against yellow fever in 1933, but whose experimental impulse during the 1940s turned to testing vaccines on humans (who, of course, were first deliberately infected with deadly diseases to measure the efficacy of the good doctor's serums). He too was given twenty years in prison. These men were highly respected in their field. While Haagen remained unrepentant, at least Bickenbach appeared personally uneasy about his role in carrying out experiments on human beings. How then do we account for the crimes they ultimately committed?

Robert Jay Lifton, a psychiatrist who documents the horrors of the death camps in his book *The Nazi Doctors: Medical Killing and the Psychology of Genocide,* has coined the term "psychic numbing" to explain how otherwise decent and law-abiding people become participants in such massive systems of evil. It essentially depends on a process of self-deception. For instance, Nazi doctors were able to carry out their murderous experiments without ever actually using the word "killing," just as animal researchers speak of "sacrificing" the creatures in their labs rather than using more honest and graphic language. Similarly, doctors in the death camps tried to justify taking the lives of prisoners by reasoning that if it was done "humanely" it presented no ethical conflict.

With tricks like these, they were able to deceive themselves about the nature and reality of their own actions.

The most troubling thing is that almost all of us are potentially subject to "psychic numbing." If Robert Jay Lifton is correct, the Nazi doctors were not monstrous characters or aberrant personalities, but ordinary physicians operating within a monstrous and aberrant environment. The evidence suggests that under the right circumstances, we too might be capable of mindless cruelty. Unless we are exceptionally strong-minded individuals, we would most likely increase the output of Milgram's voltage generator to the maximum level if directed to do so. Unless we have given careful thought to the matter beforehand, we also might very well shock the puppy, or design and carry out a similarly cruel and needless experiment like that of Sheridan and King. There the two male investigators discovered that young women were even more susceptible to browbeating than young men and concluded that because they were so prone to follow orders, girls were more likely than boys to act like fascists (one more stunning insight that animal experimentation has added to the sum of human knowledge).

But there is at least a ray of hope. For while almost all of us can be turned into bullies, none of us seems to be born that way. Like our relatives the macaques (not known as a particularly gentle or peace-loving species), we *Homo sapiens* also appear to have some inborn controls on our propensities toward violence. One of Stanley Milgram's findings was that while most people bowed to authority when asked to give the most severe shock the machine could deliver, most of them also, when given the choice to inflict either a mild or a strong shock, chose to remain on the lowest, least harmful end of the spectrum. We are not naturally sadists, it appears. We do not actually enjoy seeing other people in agony. And this means that there is nothing inherent in human nature that condemns us to replay the dismal history of what is usually called "man's inhumanity to man," but whose chief targets have usually been children, women, and other living creatures.

Consider that human sacrifice is now a thing of the past. Religious and ethical standards evolve and (in some cases) even progress. The dilemma that confronted Abraham would be unthinkable for us today, not because we are morally superior to our Hebrew ancestors but because the practice of ritualized killing has been abolished. Our instinctive inhibitions against violence are no longer tested in that particular context. And those internal restraints will continue to be strengthened to the extent that we can agree that all beings, human and non-human, have rights and interests that are deserving of respect. Perhaps someday, tormenting puppies will no longer be permitted without more careful scrutiny; confining animals in restraining devices and depriving them of food for days on end will simply not be tolerated. When that day arrives, the world will be a safer place for us all.

But to bring it to pass, we will need a new religious narrative, not one that glorifies mindless obedience and deference to authority, but rather one that encourages independent thought and dares to question the well-marked boundaries between "teacher" and "learner," experimenter and subject, human and animal, dominant and subservient. Those of us who consider ourselves people of faith might well reflect on where in our experience we find the voice of God, and what that voice might sound like. Is it the strong, confident voice of the perpetrator, who orders, directs, asserts, dictates? Is it the weak and trembling voice of the victim, who begs for mercy and forbearance? Or is it rather that calm, quiet voice within ourselves that refuses to participate in a system that narrows our choices to such stark alternatives?

Creating a safer world means cutting violence off at the root, stopping it before it has a chance to start. That means confronting it early, in schoolyard games and nursery rhymes and in the stories we tell our children. We especially need to teach nonviolence in our sacred literature, the "master stories" that guide our culture and shape our spiritual formation. How would my own childhood have been different if I had clearly learned, from earliest infancy, that it is wrong to harm another living creature? If I had been made to feel safe and protected, without a need to show a tough and menacing face to the world? I hope the lessons my children are receiving are life-giving ones. Our family does not eat meat; guns are not "toys" in our household; TV is restricted. But learning to be moral requires much more than following the rules. Sometimes it means trusting our own inner wisdom enough to upset convention. It also demands asking questions: how our behavior affects others and examining who gains, who loses, and who gets hurts as the result of our actions. As parents, my wife and I want our children to learn compassion; but empathy is acquired more through loving relationships than by obedience or submission. Nothing could be more worrisome than seeing my son or daughter display deliberate cruelty toward an animal, for that would mean that I'd somehow failed to give my children the acceptance and support that all of us need to feel a sense of our own dignity and to recognize that same quality in others.

It's when we feel deficient in ourselves that we have to make others feel small, so that we can feel big. Hitler's youth, for instance, was characterized by a consistent pattern of failures and personal defeats. National Socialism fed off the humiliation suffered by the German people following the Treaty of Versailles. When people are made to feel worthless and inferior, they tend to overcompensate by proving their superiority over others. Lacking any strong internal compass, people who depend on others for their self-affirmation can be easily manipulated and led into irrational behavior. Without confidence in their own judgment, they turn to external symbols of authority—a military uniform, a laboratory jacket—to provide the direction they find lacking in themselves.

That's how the horror starts. It begins small, with tormenting the most defenseless, but escalates in easy gradations. To stop this vicious cycle, we will need to exercise greater resistance to the voices of authority and command within our own culture, which will continue to demand more and better victims. Should living organisms be patented like mechanical inventions? Should animals be bred and engineered so their organs can be harvested for human transplant? As ethical dilemmas arise, we can expect to hear a familiar refrain. "Medical science demands ... progress requires ... research protocols insist ... you must continue ... you have no choice." Our duty in each instance will be to question the man in the lab coat, and to insist on real debate, rather than being taken in by the resonant, well-modulated voice. To be compliant is to become an accomplice.

The greatest strength of the modern animal rights movement has been its willingness to raise fundamental and far-reaching questions—questions that had been studiously ignored or considered settled beyond dispute for far too long. Who has the right to kill? A right to live? Who is a person? How far do the bounds of our moral obligation actually extend? Is it ever legitimate to use animals for medical research, or for purposes that are even less urgent? It is almost as though a long running conspiracy of silence has been broken, or as though Abraham had suddenly cast off his docile demeanor and begun to raise objections: *"What kind of God asks for the blood of the innocent, anyway?"* The answers are far from settled.

But I have faith in the questions.

꙳

The old man stood with the knife shaking in his fist. Though he had seen many springs, and offered thanks to the gods more than three score times for the lambs of a new season, it wasn't only age that made his hand tremble. It had not been steady since he had left his homeland far to the east in Ur, the land of the Chaldeans where his son was born.

Abraham thought of his son as he looked down at the tiny beast, frightened and defenseless, that was wriggling in his grip. Once it had been Isaac upon the altar, the child he had wanted so badly that he had promised its life to Molech. How many times had he prayed for an heir? How many times had he offered the burnt smoke of wild game before the image of Hadad in the temple, asking that the curse of his wife's barrenness be lifted? But no god had granted his request, not until he made that fateful bargain: his firstborn in return for descendants.

Abraham remembered the stoney silence of Sarah as he had left upon that grim errand. He recalled his son's innocence and trust as they walked together into the mountains. "Daddy, we bring the coals for the fire," Isaac had asked him. "But where is the kid for an offering?" It had been the boy's eyes that stayed his hand, the sleepy eyes that he had kissed to sleep a hundred times, the large brown eyes that lit up with delight whenever Abraham lifted him upon his shoulders.

That was when Abraham had fled from Ur to Haran, wandering with his family to Egypt, and finally settling in the remote, uncivilized hills of Canaan. He'd run for his life, for to break a vow to the god was perilous indeed. Retribution could find you anywhere, in this world or the next. That was when Abram had changed his name, to disguise his identity. It was then that he ceased paying tribute to the old deities, for he felt that he had both betrayed them and been betrayed. Abraham began to make offerings to Yahweh, the god of this new country.

And Yahweh had been good to him. Didn't the god deserve a portion of his bounty back, as a gift upon the altar? Yet Isaac had been distraught when Abraham had fastened on the beast for slaughter, pleading with him to spare its life. Though it was the youngest and the runt of the new lambs, with little chance for survival, the boy had nursed it through the first difficult weeks, protected it, and even given it a name: Angel.

Now Abraham's hand shook as he hesitated. Did he dare to tempt fate twice? The bronze blade of the knife was the same color as the iris of the animal's yellow eye, whose pupil was a dagger slit filled with terror, so different than the tearful eyes of Isaac, the reproachful eyes of Sarah, but strangely familiar too. Briefly, Abraham saw his own reflection in those liquid depths.

The eye seemed to hold a question for him. Was it possible that the animal was truly an angel, a messenger from on high? Could it be possible that this new god truly did not want or require the pungent smell of burning flesh? Did Yahweh desire compassion more than sacrifice? Or had he merely become a weak old man, afraid to follow in the footsteps of his fathers? Abraham fingered the razor's edge and looked into the little lamb's eyes again, before putting down the knife.

Chapter Four
Ask the Animals and They Will Teach You

One day the heavenly beings came to present themselves before the Lord, and Satan also came among them. The Lord said to Satan, "Where have you come from?" Satan answered the Lord, "From going to and fro on the earth, and from walking up and down on it." The Lord said to Satan, "Have you considered my servant Job? There is no one like him on the earth, a blameless and upright man who fears God and turns away from evil." Then Satan answered the Lord, "Does Job fear God for nothing? Have you not put a fence around him and his house and all that he has, on every side? You have blessed the work of his hands, and his possessions have increased in the land. But stretch out your hand now, and touch all that he has, and he will curse you to your face." The

Lord said to Satan, "Very well, all that he has is in your power; only do not stretch out your hand against him!" So Satan went out from the presence of the Lord. (Job 1:6–12)

AT TIMES THERE SEEMS TO BE A MALEVOLENT spirit at work in human affairs. The Beast. Beelzebub. Lord of the Flies. He's known by many names, this familiar figure with the cloven hoof, hairy haunches, and pointy tail. And the image of Satan walking to and fro upon the earth, scattering mischief as he goes, is a potent one. From Rwanda to the Balkans to East Timor, barbarism abounds. Mass murder . . . genocide . . . ethnic cleansing . . . such excesses of savagery hint at dark forces lurking in the shadows of our souls, creeping down the alleyways of our civilization.

In the title of a best-selling book published more than twenty-five years ago, Christian author Hal Lindsey proclaimed that *Satan Is Alive And Well On Planet Earth*. Pollster George Gallup finds that seventy-eight percent of all Americans believe in the existence of the Devil, whether as a personal or impersonal force that influences people to do evil. You might even say that if the Devil didn't exist, we would have to invent him. If not some supernatural agent, who or what is responsible for the excess of carnage we inflict on each other and the misery we bring upon ourselves?

In answering that question, it is instructive to realize that although the Devil has a fabulous and infernal history, he is actually a fairly recent invention. The earliest datable reference to Satan is in the writings of Zechariah (c. 520 BCE), but his first major Biblical appearance is in the book of Job, where spying on people, tempting them, and then waiting for them to stray from the straight and narrow are all considered part of the Evil One's job description. But the Satan we meet in Job is not precisely the Devil, only his precursor. Satan is not even his proper name. Rather it is a title, *ha-Satan*, which literally means "the Adversary" but might better be understood as the prosecuting attorney or "the Accuser." Satan is not the enemy of God, at least as pictured here. He is a member of the retinue of heavenly beings who surround and serve the Lord, just as royal ministers and attendants serve an earthly king. Satan's role may be to gather evidence against suspected sinners and rebels and put them to the test, but at all times, he acts with the consent of God, who as ruler of the universe has no real opposition.

The real Devil—the personification of evil with his easily recognizable half-human and half-animal physique—emerged later. Of course, no one knows just when Job was written. Quite archaic parallels to the story can be found throughout the ancient world. The motif of the righteous man who is the victim of injustice is apparently almost as old as the problem it poses: Why do the innocent suffer? Nevertheless, many experts think the version we know may be post-exilic, meaning that Job was composed not only in response to the general conundrum of human misery but against the background of a concrete instance of injustice, namely the Babylonian Captivity and its aftermath. During this period of forced exile, when Israel encountered the religious beliefs of its Near Eastern neighbors, the Devil began to take shape.

In 598 BCE, the kingdom of Judah had fallen to the Babylonian monarch Nebuchadnezzar, and ten years later

Jerusalem itself was leveled after a siege where, according to the book of Lamentations, starving women were reduced to boiling their own children for food. The Israelite king Jehoiachim and leading citizens were deported, and none would be permitted to return to their homeland for another fifty years, until the Babylonian empire fell to the Persian king Cyrus, whose policy of religious tolerance permitted the refugees to be repatriated. The Jewish people had to ask why God had allowed such a catastrophe to happen. And the answers they deduced were inevitably influenced by the religions of Babylon and Persia, their conquerors and liberators. For at about the same time Israel was taken captive, a new teacher named Zoroaster appeared in the East.

Zoroaster taught that the universe was a battlefield between the forces of light and darkness—purest good and absolute evil. Ahura Mazda and Ahriman were the names of the two opposing deities who, Zoroaster said, had been at war since the beginning of time. And human beings were participants in this cosmic battle. For with each thought, word, and deed, men and women aligned themselves either with the force of good or its opposite. One day, Zoroaster believed, Ahura Mazda would send a savior down to earth who would finally defeat the kingdom of darkness and bring an end to time. Then the dead would be resurrected and tried at a last judgment. And then the righteous would live for all eternity in Paradise, while the wicked would be consigned to a realm of endless punishment.

Whoever wrote Job may have been influenced by the metaphysical dualism of these doctrines. Aramaic was the official language of the Persian empire, where Zoroaster lived (his religion was practiced in the royal court there), and the numerous Aramaic phrases in Job lead some critics to think the text must have been composed in a region where Persian culture predominated. Yet "the Adversary" we find in Job is no rival to the singular authority of God. The idea of Satan as God's nemesis would not become fully developed until New Testament times.

While precise lines of influence are hard to establish, the gospels tell us that "wise men from the East" were present at the birth of Jesus. These *Magi*, at least if we can trust the testimony of the Greek chronicler Herodotus, were Zoroastrian priests. Whether the stories of the nativity in Bethlehem can be taken as historical records is doubtful, but they do seem to preserve a memory that Christianity was infused with Persian mythology at its very inception, born of the confluence of cultures that merged when Persia fell to Alexander the Great. In the coming together of East and West, the faith of Zoroaster met the Greek philosophy of Alexander's famous tutor, Aristotle. And we are still living with the aftereffects of that encounter.

Aristotle, as we have seen, taught that the universe is arranged hierarchically. Since the heavens are literally higher than the earth, in a spatial as well as a normative sense, man actually "stands above" the other animals, not only in height but in rank. "For of all animals man alone stands erect, in accordance with his godlike nature and essence," wrote Aristotle in *On the Parts of Animals*. "For it is the function of the god-like to think and be wise; and no easy task were this under the burden of a heavy body, pressing down from above and obstructing by its weight the motions of the intellect and the general sense." All other animals are dwarf-like in form, the philosopher maintained, and like human dwarves or infants that crawled upon the ground, had a larger admixture of "earthy matter" in their constitutions and less of "elevating heat," rendering them naturally inferior to those with an upright posture. While plants might appear to grow upwards and thereby contradict the generalization that height automatically ennobles, Aristotle explained that plants in fact grow upside down—their roots correspond to the heads of animals, since this is where their "nutritive" organs are located—and so they only serve to prove the rule that higher is better.

Yet even plants possessed a "vegetative soul," Aristotle said, and in this he was merely systematizing and restating the popular consensus of the pagan world that nature was alive and endowed with a spiritual principle. Great gods and goddesses like Zeus and Demeter embodied the energies present in such natural marvels as thunder and lightning or the changing of the seasons. Major deities like these had their own rites, cults, and temples. But every hill and stream and valley was believed in Greco-Roman times to possess its own distinctive *daimon* or animating spirit. And more thoughtful individuals in the pagan world, long after they had abandoned a naive belief in the pantheon of Greece or Rome, felt that all these diverse *daimones* were merely expressions of a single *anima mundi* or "world soul." As Marcus Aurelius wrote:

> *Cease not to think of the Universe as one, living Being, possessed of a single substance and a single soul . . . and how all existing things are joint causes of all things that come into existence; and how intertwined in the fabric is the thread, and how closely woven the web.*

Nature itself was a focus of reverence and meditation.

But nature was "denatured" and the *daimones* became demons as the hierarchical world of Aristotle was infected with the dualistic tendencies of Zoroaster and his successors. The pagan image of the world as an intertwined fabric and closely woven web was replaced with the new picture of a universe torn by neverending conflict between light and dark, man and nature, matter and spirit. Matter, including the body and all the carnal aspects of our being, came to be looked upon as an impediment or even prison house, confining the soul and hindering its ascent to an ethereal or celestial plane. (Under Platonic influence, *sōma*, the Greek word for body, became linked with *sēma*, the term for prison.) Women were condemned for giving birth to the gross anatomy of our physical existence. (Tertullian, one of the early Church Fathers, called women "the devil's gateway.") And nature, especially other living creatures, came to be regarded as incarnations of everything base, ignoble and contrary to the finer impulses of our humanity—diabolical rather than divine.

Through the ages the figure of the Devil has come to be a repository of all those unsavory aspects that we wish to disassociate ourselves from and project onto others. And in this connection it is interesting to note that one of the most frequently used scriptural designations for the Devil, almost as common as Satan, is "Belial," which can be translated as "the Worthless One," a distillation of all we find distasteful or negative in our own experience. In some ancient texts, for instance, Satan is called "the Black One" and described as a swarthy Ethiopian; so the Lord of Darkness becomes an amalgam of racial fears and prejudices. But antipathy toward animals is even stronger than hostility based on race. Thus the Devil is typically depicted in animal form, his goat-like features apparently borrowed from the Greek god Pan, the *daimon* of pastures, flocks, and forests. The "scapegoat" of Hebrew tradition—an animal that was driven into the wilderness to carry away to burden of blame for a people's unwanted sins—may also have contributed to the Devil's mien, from horns to goatee. *Brutish*, *bestial*, and *animalistic* would become virtual synonyms for whatever was degenerate or morally depraved. Comparing one's enemies to beasts or vermin—the more loathsome the better—became a convenient excuse for unleashing one's own malicious and aggressive impulses in wars, crusades and other forms of persecution. For so long as we see the world as a struggle between absolutes of right and wrong, we can justify the total annihilation of others while still claiming purity for ourselves. When we begin to separate people into saved and unsaved (or sheep and goats), all manner of madness becomes possible.

If our negative view of animals has deep psychological roots, it also has disturbing psychological consequences. According to Boris Levinson, the founder of Animal Assisted Therapy:

> *One of the chief reasons for man's present difficulties is his inability to come to terms with his inner self and to harmonize his culture with his membership in the world of nature. Rational man has become alienated from himself by refusing to face his irrational self, his own past as personified by animals.*

We are animals, but at the same time we despise animals, an emotional contradiction that has its costs. For the denial and repression of our own animal nature represents a form of self-hatred: a rejection of our own being. The resulting rage can be directed either inward, in the form of depression, shame, and guilt, or outward, as aggression toward others. But the original contradiction cannot be resolved, Levinson argued, until we restore a healing connection to our own unconscious animal natures by establishing positive relationships with other living creatures.

Such "animal assisted" healing really does take place—at least if we can believe the book of Job. For in response to the misfortunes that have been visited on him—the loss of all he holds dear—Job persistently asks that he be allowed to question the Almighty. Of the several epiphanies in the Bible—those rare occasions when the Holy manifests its own presence whether to Moses in a burning bush or to Isaiah in a vision of the throne room of the divine—God's self-revelation in Job is the most lengthy and most complete. And it is through nature—the wheeling of the constellations, the surging of the sea, and above all the wonder and diversity of living creatures who populate our planet—that God chooses to be known.

In the closing chapters of Job, God asks Job to contemplate the amazing array of species who have sprung from the womb of creation. Most scholars agree that this entire passage was crafted by a different hand than the one that wrote the book's opening, where God and Satan strike their fateful bargain. The style and diction are entirely different and so is the author's attitude toward other creatures. Far from being considered chattel or possessions, animals here are regarded as representatives of realities that can never be possessed. The lioness with her young, the mountain goats giving birth, the calving deer, the ostrich who trusts the earth to warm her eggs to bring them to parturition, the eagle and the raven who scour the land to satisfy the appetites of their nestlings: all are rendered in beautiful imagery as instances of the generative, feminine, and nurturing mysteries of life. Then there are also the wild ox that resists human domestication ("Is the wild ox willing to serve you? Will it spend the night at your crib? Can you tie it in the furrow with ropes, or will it harrow the valleys after you?"); the hippopotamus heedless of the fisherman's hooks and snares (called "the first of the great acts of God"), at rest in the reedy marsh beneath the fragrant lotus; the fearless stallion who charges his foes to ground and the vulture in his high eerie: these speak of a sacred order which exists prior to humankind, primordial and independent of civilized values. "You have asked me to show myself," God seemingly says to Job, "and in the most elemental and sensuous acts of nature I stand revealed." And that answer is strangely satisfying to Job. His loss becomes bearable. His anger and resentment are dissipated. He comes to a deeper understanding of the world that reconciles him to life, with all its grief.

What brings him to this new place of acceptance and peace? Perhaps it was the same process of healing and transformation that Jane Goodall experienced after the tragic death of her husband, Derek Bryceson. His diagnosis of colon cancer in 1979 marked the beginning of a descent into darkness and soul-searching for the famous primatologist. In spite of her prayers, the doctors found her husband's condition to be inoperable and gave Derek only weeks to live. Those few weeks were wracked with anguish. "The gradual increase of pain, the injections at night instead of the pills," she wrote as she watched her husband dying in agony. "Oh the horror, the horror of it . . . .Suffering for the suffering of one I loved ever more deeply with each passing day." Like Job, Goodall looked everywhere for answers: to Western medicine, to God's mercy, to faith healers, to psychics, but nothing seemed to slow the terrible disease. And like Job, she came to a point of doubt, when she could no longer make sense of what was happening. "And so, for a while after Derek's death, I rejected God, and the world seemed a bleak place."

It was a year and a half later, says Goodall in her autobiography, that hope once more entered her universe, through an epiphany not so different from that described in the book of Job. She had traveled back to Gombe, on the shores of Lake Tanganyika, after weeks of lecturing in America. At home again with her beloved chimpanzees, she found herself caught together with them in a drenching rainstorm, then basking in the soft glow of sunlight that followed. "It is hard—impossible, really—to put into words the moment of truth that suddenly came upon me then," she says. "Even the mystics are unable to describe their brief flashes of spiritual ecstasy."

It seemed to me, as I struggled afterward to recall the experience, that self was utterly absent: I and the chimpanzees, the earth and trees and air, seemed to merge, to become one with the spirit power of life itself. The air was filled with a feathered symphony, the evensong of birds. I heard new frequencies in their music and also in the singing insects' voices—notes so high and sweet I was amazed.

Each leaf on every tree seemed indescribably rich in shape and shading, with a delicate tracery of veins forming a pattern that was individual and unlike any other. The fragrances of the soaking forest mingled in a heady perfume, yet every odor remained distinct: the scents of moist earth and the moldering aroma of decaying, overripe fruits, the loamy smell of damp bark, along with her own wet tresses and the steaming hair of the chimpanzees. The sweetness of crushed vegetation was intoxicating. She sensed rather than saw another presence, then looked upwind to spy a magnificent bushbuck quietly feeding, with spiraled horns shimmering in the luminous air. Goodall felt at that moment that she was part of a natural order that "dwarfs and yet somehow enhances human emotions." She realized in a powerful and visceral way that she was connected to a Reality that held all life within its embrace, bringing her a sense of serenity and strength she had never known before. The forest had given her, she says, "the peace that passes understanding."

Goodall's experience reminds me of the ending of the book of Job. After being taken on a tour of the world's fauna—from the wild ass to the crocodile—with God as the tour guide, Job sits down in the dust, wonderstruck at all he's seen.

> *I know that you can do all things*
> *and that no purpose of yours can be thwarted.*
> *Therefore I have uttered what I did not understand,*
> *things too wonderful for me, which I did not know …*
> *I had heard of you by the hearing of the ear,*
> *but now my eye sees you.*

As a result of this transforming encounter with nature, Job is a changed man, and his next words are revealing. The phrase he utters is usually translated "I despise myself," but this is misleading. Job is not having self-esteem problems or indulging in a bout of self-hatred. He is describing something quite different. His words would be better rendered as "I melt away" (the preferred wording in the *New English Bible*) or as "I melt away into nothing," which the *Revised Standard Version* offers in its annotations to the text. Job's old *persona* is dissolving.

Job appears to be describing a traditional religious experience in which the boundaries of the ego become porous. His identity, which he had previously confused with his skin-encapsulated self, has been expanded to include a much larger domain. The circle of his being and belonging is no longer limited to his own immediate family or personal fortune. He has gained a sense of sympathetic inter-relation with the entire earth community, if not the entire cosmos.

As in Jane Goodall's account, where "I and the chimpanzees, the earth and trees and air, seemed to merge," Job has become incorporated into a larger life. And entry into that larger life replaces his private torment with a sense of unity and peace.

"All My Relations" is a phrase that many Native Americans use to describe this sense of interconnection with the earth and its creatures. And these were also the words that Louise Diamond employed to describe her own journey of rebirth, as I listened to her speak in the living room of a friend. Diagnosed with breast cancer, Louise had her first mastectomy at the age of twenty-eight. A few months later a tumor appeared in her other breast. With such a recurrence, doctors told her, her chances were nil. The odds of recovery were practically zero. Recently divorced and a single mother with an energetic toddler, Louise felt her world collapsing. "I remember when the hysteria set in. Shortly after I returned from the hospital after the second operation, I received a birth announcement in the mail. My instinctive reaction was, 'It's not fair! How can my friends be celebrating new life when I'm preparing for death?'"

If she was going to die, Louise decided, she wanted to leave the world in beauty. So she decided to immerse herself in nature. She began to wander the backwoods and roam the untrodden trails of New England, and she began to notice small details that had earlier escaped her attention, the shapes and sizes and varieties of flowers, for instance. She also observed that every flower, no matter what its color or fragrance, had a center. "I began to ask how I might be like the flower. Did I have a center? If so, what or where was it? What was the relationship between my center and a flower's center?" Observing the numerous species of trees in the forests and orchards—the slender birches, stately pines, and gnarled but tenacious apples—she also saw that every one grew in two directions, up and down, sending roots into the nourishing earth and lifting leaves and branches high into the air. "What were my roots?" she asked. "What parts of me stretched up to meet the sun, to dance within the light?" For four years, Louise spent as much time as possible among the marshy spots and muddy places with only beaver, muskrat, and dragonflies as companions. And from that sojourn in the wilderness, she discovered that the Native American concept of "All My Relations" was more than a metaphor. It was also a potent force for healing, making what was broken whole.

With her health restored, Louise decided to put her hard won insights into practice. She found a new vocation, training herself as a specialist in international conflict resolution, working in places like Bosnia, Cyprus, and the Middle East.

In her book *The Courage for Peace*, she shares her finding that violent conflict usually has multiple causes. At the global level, many of the causes are tangible: economic dislocation, territorial disputes, or the ravages of a regional arms race. But strife almost always has a spiritual aspect as well, as the combatants fall into familiar and all-too-habitual modes of thought: scapegoating, blaming, and demonizing the other, projecting their own fear and malice onto the face of the enemy, and falsely imagining that every conflict can be reduced to a simple contest of Right versus Wrong. Unfortunately, these destructive patterns seem to have a fiendish hold on the human mind. You could even say they have been giving us the Devil for over two thousand years.

Hatred destroys everyone it touches, not least of all those whom it inflames and embitters. Racism blights the soul of the white hatemonger, as well as injecting misery and dread into the lives of people of color. Sexism diminishes men, who find themselves trapped in narrow stereotypes of masculinity, quite as much as it limits the aspirations of women. And speciesism—the ideology of human domination—can poison our spirits just like other forms of bigotry and oppression. For this is the root of what is truly demonic in human existence—elevating the part above the whole, so that membership in a particular nation or clan, gender or species becomes the final measure of all worth.

Sexism and speciesism, xenophobia and homophobia—aren't they all related? My newspaper recently carried a story about a man in Florida, for instance, who had been arrested for fatally beating a dog because he thought the animal was "gay." Upset when his wife's neutered male mixed-breed expressed interest in another male, a Jack Russell terrier, the assailant hit the animal in the head with a vacuum cleaner and then hurled it against tree until it lapsed into a coma. It would be hard to say who was the more damaged of the two—the dog who died or the man whose identity was so conflicted that he was threatened and driven to violence by such innocent canine behavior. Something inside the killer had become severely torn and twisted. But, to a lesser degree, don't we all bear the scars that come from living in an abusive relationship with nature? This inward ambivalence allows us to dote on creatures that are pets or especially favored while subjecting others to unspeakable indignities. We both idealize animals and are repulsed by them, in an unhealthy brew of enmity and affection. But so long as we remain inwardly divided— denying and decrying what is creaturely in our own nature—our inner conflicts will continue to spill over into our relationships with others. Discord will be the result.

Will we ever find "the peace that passes understanding?" Letting go of old wounds, overcoming ancient animosities, and finding balm for the grievances and injuries that mar the unity of creation will demand new habits of thought. We must stop imagining that hierarchies exist where nature shows only difference. We can no longer divide the world into friend and foe, but must realize that all the earth's inhabitants form one family. We are all related—all nations and all species—from the DNA within our cells to the hopes within our hearts. We share a common origin and a single destiny. But where can we look for teachers? How can we become more sensitive to the reality of our interdependence? The book of Job offers this insight:

> *Ask the animals, and they will teach you;*
> *the birds of the air, and they will tell you;*
> *ask the plants of the earth, and they will teach you;*
> *and the fish of the sea will declare to you.*
> *Who among all these does not know that the hand of the Lord*
>   *has done this?*
> *In his hand is the life of every living thing*
> *and the breath of every human being.* (Job 12:7–10)

Animal liberation can lead to human liberation—freeing us from partial identities and restricted loyalties, opening us to sympathy with all that live. One Hasidic rabbi put it this way: "When you walk across the fields with your mind pure and holy, then from all the stones, and all the growing things, and all animals, the sparks of their soul come out and cling to you, and then they are purified and become a holy fire in you."

A vibrant sense of kinship with other living beings is the "holy fire" that can heal our brokenness, restoring us to right relationship with ourselves, our neighbors, and our world.

ℵ

> *Then God spoke to him from out of the whirlwind*
>   *(or so it seemed),*
> *For Job felt both fear and exhilaration*
> *At the power that bent the branches of cypress and olive*

Like slender grasses, making them dance
As dervishes dance, whose whirling is also a prayer.
And Job bent too and swayed before the gale,
Surrendering himself to the storm with a strange gladness.
All night Job kept watch
At the dark clouds scudding across the moon,
A silver disc dimmed and then illumined
But always present, whether hidden or revealed.
And many times Job passed from waking into dream,
Until he was unsure which was which,
So vivid were the images cast upon his inward eye
And so haunting the intonations.
"Where were you when I created the heavens and the earth?"
An insistent voice demanded, though where it originated,
From elsewhere or within, Job could not say.
Nor could its accents be placed,
For it seemed both young and old,
Reminding Job of his mother's voice and his grandfather's too,
And of the murmuring of many waters
And the sighing of beasts
And the sound of insects droning.
"Have you entered into the springs of the sea?
Or have you walked in search of the depths?"
The voice quizzed Job,
And the question itself contained such depths
As Job had never known existed,
A doorway opening into unexpected interiors.
"Where were you when I hung the lights:
Arcturus and Orion, the Great Bear and his brother?"

And from high in the heavens, Job glimpsed the earth,
A dot of blue amid the immensities of space,
Vulnerable and lovely and small.
"Have you given the horse his strength,
Or clothed his neck with thunder?"
With that, a strength not his own flowed into Job
As the voice multiplied question upon question
("Who gave the eagle his wings?")
("What lasts longer than the mountains?")
Until their sum was a mystery
Past finding out,
Beyond any intelligible answer,
But to which Job's soul responded "Yes."
And when the storm had passed and morning came again
The sun rose upon Job with a light as rich as on the first day
When all the sons of God sang together
And the daughters of the Most High shouted with joy.
The rain had washed away Job's anger.
His tears had cleaned the mire from his eyes.
"I repent," said Job, with a great letting go,
And the bitterness and hurt were gone,
The old querulousness had departed—where?
Where does a hard knot go when the soft cord's come
        unloosened?
Then Job sat down in the dust
And let the fine grit run through his fingers,
Knowing that the common mud was his own substance,
Accepting his place within the family of things.

Chapter Five
The Belly of the Beast

Jonah prayed to the Lord his God from the belly of the fish, saying:

"I called to the Lord out of my distress, and he answered
me;
out of the belly of Sheol I cried, and you heard my voice.
You cast me into the deep, into the heart of the seas,
and the flood surrounded me;
all your waves and your billows passed over me.
Then I said, 'I am driven away from your sight;
how shall I look again upon your holy temple?'
The waters closed in over me; the deep surrounded me;
weeds were wrapped around my head at the roots
of the mountains.
I went down to the land whose bars closed upon me
forever;
yet you brought up my life from the Pit,
O Lord my God.

As my life was ebbing away, I remembered the Lord;
　　and my prayer came to you, into your holy temple.
Those who worship vain idols forsake their true loyalty.
But I with the voice of thanksgiving will sacrifice to you;
　　what I have vowed I will pay.
Deliverance belongs to the Lord!"
Then the Lord spoke to the fish, and it spewed Jonah out upon
the dry land. (Jonah 2:1–10)

NATURE MOVES IN CIRCLES AND THIS IS beautiful. People straighten the curves and that is Progress. The difference was driven home for me on a recent visit to the Everglades. Our family spent a morning canoeing through the saw grass and mangrove swamps where the current curved back on itself like the whorls of the Apple Snails whose shells were everywhere. The entire Everglades are in fact a slowly moving river and a biological marvel, the first National Park created for the diversity of its life forms rather than its scenic splendor. But to reach the canoe trails one must first drive "Alligator Alley," the highway that runs straight as a ruler across the breadth of Florida, past the irrigation channels that also divide the peninsula into a rectangular grid of countless citrus farms. Today the park is threatened by these straight chutes of progress. The water that sustains this ecological wonderland is no longer permitted to meander its circuitous way toward the Florida Bay.

Progress in ethics is also better measured by a widening circle than by a straight line. As our moral community expands from members of our immediate family to others in our clan, tribe, and nation, the perimeter widens until the circle of our concern finally extends to include all creation. "To the primitive," as Albert

Schweitzer observed in his book *The Teaching of Reverence for Life*, "solidarity has narrow limits." At his jungle hospital in Lambaréné, Schweitzer would sometimes ask an ambulatory patient to fetch a glass of water or undertake some other small service for another inmate who was still confined to bed. But frequently the response was: "This man is not my brother." Unless the two were related ethnically, rendering assistance was out of the question. But at some point in our moral development, as we begin to reflect on ourselves and our relationship to others, Schweitzer says, our sense of kinship begins to grow.

Schweitzer, a professor of theology and known for his Biblical scholarship as much as for his idealism and service to others, pointed to such moral growth in the religion of ancient Israel. The God of Abraham and Isaac—a familial and tribal deity—was universalized by prophets like Amos, Hosea, and Isaiah into One whose sense of equity and fairness applies equally to all people. The same affirmation of human unity can be found in other faiths, Schweitzer noted: in the teachings of Jesus, in the tenets of Confucius, and in Buddhism as well.

Jonah stands in the line of the Hebrew prophets, but carries their message one step farther, toward its logical conclusion. For while Jonah is grouped among the so-called "minor" prophets, his story marks a major advance among Biblical authors in terms of concern for animals. Some consider Jonah a parody. But despite its ironies, Jonah has a serious message to deliver, and though one of the shortest books in the Bible, the story is long on meaning.

The outline is simple enough. Jonah is commanded by God to pronounce an indictment against the wicked city of Nineveh. For reasons we learn later, Jonah defies God and tries to run away, boarding a ship headed for Tarshish, in the opposite direction. When a wild storm threatens to swamp the craft, the sailors cast lots to discover which person on board is responsible for the tempest and learn of Jonah's evasion. Although the mariners do their best to row for safety, they can see it is no use. Reluctantly, and at Jonah's own suggestion, they finally toss the runaway prophet into the waves to quiet the raging sea.

Jonah is then swallowed by a "large fish" and spends three days and three nights inside the belly of the monster before being belched back onto dry land, at which point God again demands that he carry a message to Nineveh. When he at last arrives in the city (so large that it takes him three days to walk across it), Jonah warns the inhabitants that the Lord is angry and about to destroy their mighty metropolis. Immediately, the king calls his subjects to repentance, and not only the citizens of Nineveh but also their animals begin to fast from both food and drink, dressed in sackcloth.

Jonah is angry when God extends forgiveness to the Ninevites. He would have preferred to see the city destroyed, without warning them of their peril. For Nineveh was the capital of Assyria, the very empire that had annihilated the northern kingdom of Israel some years before and turned its people into the ten "lost tribes." "That is why I fled to Tarshish at the beginning; for I knew that you are a gracious God and merciful, slow to anger, and abounding in steadfast love, and ready to relent from punishing." Seeing Nineveh saved, Jonah stomps madly into the desert, preferring to die rather than live with such an unwelcome outcome.

God then sends a bush to grow over Jonah, to save him from the withering heat. The prophet is grateful for the shade, but the next day the Lord makes the bush shrivel away, and Jonah once more expresses a bitter wish that his life might end. In conclusion, God issues Jonah a divine reprimand:

> *You are concerned about the bush, for which you did not labor and which you did not grow; it came into being in a night and perished in a night. And should I not be concerned about Nineveh, that great city, in which there are more than a hundred and twenty thousand persons who do not know their right hand from their left, and also many animals?*
> (Jonah 3:10–11)

The circle widens as our sense of solidarity grows. As Schweitzer says: "We begin to perceive that ethics deals not only with people, but also with creatures." The God who spares Nineveh, not only for the sake of its two-legged citizens, but also for its many animals, represents an enlightened advance in this respect. Jonah demonstrates concern for the whole family of humankind and not solely for a chosen few, whether Jew or gentile. Both the crew of the ship that ferries Jonah toward Tarshish and the inhabitants of Nineveh—pagans though they be—seem morally admirable compared to the petulant title character. Yet the book goes on to express God's care, not only for human beings of all faiths and races, but for other species as well.

Few books of the Bible are better known than Jonah, or more misunderstood. Many misread the narrative as nothing more than a glorified fish story, trying to prove that the prophet's long weekend inside the whale might really have occurred. One account that has been cited frequently in the search for modern parallels involves a sailor named James Bartley and a whaling ship called *Star of the East*, which supposedly cruised the South Atlantic near the Falkland Islands sometime in the 1890s. When a sperm whale was sighted, the vessel lowered its harpoon boats, which were carried a considerable distance after spearing the creature. In the ensuing meleé, one of the boats capsized, and Bartley was presumed drowned when he could not be located among the survivors. After the whale had finally been killed and secured to the side of the ship, the crew began the laborious process of stripping away the blubber, working with their knives all through the day and night and into the next morning before they finally reached the stomach. Through the wall of the distended organ, they noticed spasmodic signs of life, and when the contents of the stomach were examined, there was James Bartley, doubled-over and unconscious. When he was finally able to speak again, Bartley recounted the strange story from an insider's point of view.

> *He says that he remembers the sensation of being lifted into the air by the nose of the whale and dropping into the water. Then there was a frightful rushing sound, which he believed to be the beating of the water by the whale's tail, then he was encompassed by a fearful darkness, and he felt himself slipping along a smooth passage of some sort that seemed to move and carry him forward. This sensation lasted but an instant, then he felt that he had more room. He felt about him, and his*

hands came in contact with a yielding slimy substance that seemed to shrink from his touch. It finally dawned upon him that he had been swallowed by a whale, and he was overcome with horror at the situation. He could breathe, but the heat was terrible. It was not of a scorching, stifling nature, but it seemed to draw out his vitality . . . and he must have fainted, for the next he remembered was being in the captain's cabin.

Most accounts say that Bartley was "a raving lunatic" immediately after his rescue, but gradually recovered his senses. While his skin remained bleached from the gastric juices inside the whale's gut, there were no other lasting effects from his ordeal.

The story is probably a fabrication. In attempting to authenticate the legend, Edward David, a professor of science and history at Messiah College, discovered there was no James Bartley listed on the crew manifest for the voyage in question. The captain's wife, moreover, stated flatly that "I was with my husband all the years he was in the *Star of the East*. There was never a man lost overboard while my husband was in her. The sailor has told a great sea yarn."

Yet the tale of the man who was swallowed by a whale has been repeated and reprinted frequently, in religious tracts and various Bible commentaries. The thought of being eaten alive seems to have a persistent hold on the religious imagination, regardless of its literal truth. One could call this gruesome image of being ingested—incorporated in one gulp into the body of another being—an *archetype*, a recurring theme that seems to hold some hidden significance for the human psyche.

The image first appears in the Babylonian myth called *Enuma Elish*, tentatively dated to the early second millennium BCE but possibly based on much older Sumerian sources. *Enuma Elish* derives its name from its opening words, "When On High." This epic tells how the world was created when Marduk, a storm god, defeated the primeval chaos personified by the goddess Tiamat, who threatened to swallow him through her enormous maw:

> *When Tiamat opened her mouth to destroy him,*
> *He sent in the Evil Wind, so that she could not close her lips.*
> *The raging winds filled her belly,*
> *Her body was distended and her mouth gaped.*

Driving the winds down Tiamat's gullet, Marduk then shoots an arrow clean through her stomach and divides her body to form the earth and sky.

Echoes of *Enuma Elish* can be heard in Genesis, which like its Babylonian counterpart begins with a temporal clause, "*When....*" When God begins to create the heavens and the earth, darkness covers the face of the deep, while a mighty wind sweeps over the waters. *Tehom*, the Hebrew word for "deep," is etymologically related to *Tiamat*, and like Marduk, God drives a wind over the abyss, dividing and separating the inchoate waters, those above the dome of heaven from those below, to begin the work of creation. Elsewhere in scripture, intimations of a mythic contest between God and a prehistoric denizen of the deep are evoked more explicitly, as in Psalm 74:

> *You divided the sea by your might;*

you broke the heads of the dragons in the waters.
You crushed the heads of Leviathan . . .

Here the monster is identified as sea serpent. And this is also the image we meet in Jonah, who is cast into the deep and cries out from the belly of Sheol. There is no point speculating whether the "large fish" that swallowed the reluctant prophet was a whale, a whale shark, or some other species large and hungry enough to consume a human snack. Jonah's terrifying trip into the belly of the beast is a mythological journey, not a gastronomical one.

The archetypal fear of being swallowed whole resurfaces in Christian art. Jesus is depicted, in some early images, impaled upon a crucifix curved and barbed like a fishhook. The Devil, in the form of a large fish, greedily eyes this delectable morsel and prepares to take the bait. Augustine, in a slight variation, likens Jesus to the lure inside a mousetrap. (The iconography here is intended as an explanation of the atonement. When Satan snatches away the life of Christ, which is innocent and therefore not rightfully his, he must give up his claim to the lives of sinners he would otherwise be entitled to, as a *quid pro quo*.) In the sixteenth century, the paintings of Brueghel the Elder rendered scenes of the Last Judgment in terrifying pictorial detail, showing long lines of the damned marching into the huge mouth of a fish-like creature as large as a house, who gobbles the wretched souls down a throat as dark and menacing as death. A woodcut by Matthias Gerung, from the same era, is even more startling. Five diners are seated around a board, decked with tablecloth, plates and cups, preparing to share a meal. But the entire supper club sits within the mouth of a gargantuan fiend, ready to devour them whole. The scene is a satire on the practice of selling indulgences; presumably, the doomed gourmands have purchased permission to feast when they should be fasting. In any case, the diners have become the dinner.

The archetype seems to draw its power from the disturbing realization that life exists only by consuming other life—a thought that most of us prefer to hold at arm's length. But it was apparent to me, canoeing in Florida among the alligators with their gently smiling jaws. Even though a ranger told us that only one attack had ever been documented in the fifty year history of Everglades National Park, when a tourist inadvertently rode his bicycle over one of the cold-blooded animals, I was careful to keep my distance. For whether we happen to be at the top or bottom, all of us are part of the food chain. Even people who survive closest to nature, like the Eskimo, seldom make the complete connection. The ethnographer Knud Rasmussen quoted one Iglulik man as saying:

> The greatest peril of life lies in the fact that human food consists entirely of souls. All the creatures that we have to kill and eat, all those that we have to strike down and destroy to make clothes for ourselves, have souls, like we have, souls that do not perish with the body, and which must therefore be propitiated.

What is left unsaid is that we too are made of flesh and one day will be eaten in turn. Almost every religion has ritualized mechanisms for addressing this conundrum. Eating becomes a sacrament in many traditions, as in Judaism, where the dietary laws (or *kashrut*) are explained as spiritual opportunities—possibilities for participating in the holiness of creation. But by the same token, being eaten remains a source of existential anxiety. The motif of the gaping mouth, engulfing us in our entirety, encapsulates our fear that there is a deadly contradiction in the very bowels of life.

Over time, the dread of Leviathan affixed itself to real whales, who are not nearly as horrifying as the existential dilemmas they seem to symbolize. When Captain Scammon first sailed into the lagoon of Baja California that now bears his name, he discovered the inlet was filled with gray whales. He immediately lowered his boats to begin hunting them. Finding themselves under attack, the whales retaliated by smashing the vessels of their tormenters. This caused Baja whalers to christen the gray whale the "Devil Fish" for its murderous behavior. Other species, like the sperm whale Melville seized upon as an emblem of evil in his novel *Moby Dick* and the orca or killer whale, were even more feared. For a time the U.S. Navy considered killer whales so dangerous that official policy required all small boats to be removed from the water if orcas were in the vicinity.

But while whales do act in self-defense when necessary, their reputation for ferocity is undeserved. Killer whales eat fish, seals, and walruses, but have never been known to munch on *Homo sapiens*. And now the so-called "Devil Fish" has become known as a gentle giant. Soon after whale-watching excursions began to catch on in the 1960s, the gray whales of the lagoons in Baja California began to behave in a very unexpected manner. They started to actively approach the boats to float alongside them as sightseers stroked and patted their massive heads, rolling over occasionally to have their bellies rubbed as well. That led to even more close encounters. "We already know that every species of whale with which anyone has swum is normally peaceful," says Roger Payne, who has spent his life studying cetaceans, "careful to avoid hitting the clumsy and helpless human swimmers around it with its flukes." Accidents do happen, but the rare bumps and bruises almost always come from calves who are still uncoordinated and lack fine motor control. Of course, whales have little reason to inflict injury on creatures they must regard as pipsqueaks, who pose no possible threat. A whale that becomes annoyed with rubbernecking tourists can easily dive or swim away. Still, the restraint these animals show toward humans, who could be crushed so casually, is remarkable.

Such friendly interactions may be leading us toward a new paradigm in our relationship with other creatures, says Payne, who is currently president of the Whale Conservation Institute. Perhaps most species are more hospitably disposed toward people than we have previously imagined. Whales and other marine mammals have been comparatively protected from human encroachment by their watery environment. And while land animals have had millennia to learn to mistrust humankind, ocean dwellers may see us more as a curiosity than a threat. Many of these creatures, like dolphins, seem positively drawn to our kind in playful goodwill. "I have the feeling that where animals have not learned from firsthand experience to fear us, they are usually prepared to greet humanity in peace," writes Payne in *Among Whales*. "It would seem to follow that the wildness of animals may well be a creation of our approach to them rather than of theirs to us. It is not necessarily a propensity with which they are born.

From which it would follow that in order to live in peace with the wild world, we need only change how we present ourselves to it."

Jonah (whose name in Hebrew means "dove," providing a clue to his message) could be taken as a forerunner of this new attitude. For the important thing to notice about the book is not that a whale swallows Jonah, but rather that a whale saves him from drowning and delivers him to shore. "The Lord provided a large fish," according to the text, and "it spewed Jonah out upon the dry land." The fearsome Leviathan has been completely transformed from a figure of destruction to the agent of deliverance. Could these creatures again provide an answer to our prayers? As Roger Payne remarks, the challenge now awaiting humankind is not so much to "save the whales" as to be saved by them—helped toward a new appreciation and sense of partnership with other living beings.

Schweitzer had his own name for this deepened sense of relatedness. He called it "Reverence for Life." It was a realization that came to him as he floated upriver on a mission of mercy, summoned from the coast at Cape Lopez to treat the wife of a colleague at N'Gômô over a hundred and fifty miles inland. The year was 1913 and he had been traveling three days. "Lost in thought I sat on the deck of the barge, struggling to find the elementary and universal conception of the ethical which I had not discovered in any philosophy." Dissatisfied with the ethical systems of the past—traditions that set the human species against and apart from nature—Schweitzer relates that he was seeking the basis for a morality that would be genuinely life-affirming. It was at the precise moment when the boat passed through a herd of hippopotami that the kindly doctor had his epiphany.

Schweitzer's autobiography doesn't record whether he looked into the cavernous mouths of these creatures whom the Bible calls "Behemoth," cousin to the mighty Leviathan. But he clearly looked straight down the throat of the philosophical problem they seemed to represent. As a physician, Schweitzer was well aware of the trade-offs of birth and death. The life of a microbe might have to be eradicated to gain the life of a child. Life does exist at the expense of other life. "I buy from natives a young fish eagle, which they have caught on a sandbank, in order to rescue it from their cruel hands," reflected Schweitzer. "But now I have to decide whether I shall let it starve, or kill every day a number of small fishes, in order to keep it alive."

> *Standing, as he does, with the whole body of living creatures under the law of this dilemma . . . man comes again and again into the position of being able to preserve his own life and life generally only at the cost of other life. If he has been touched by the ethic of Reverence for Life, he injures and destroys life only under a necessity which he cannot avoid, and never from thoughtlessness. So far as he is a free man he uses every opportunity of tasting the blessedness of being able to assist life and avert from it suffering and destruction.*

Like Jonah, we are all in the belly of the beast, trapped in the seemingly inescapable situation that we share with every other organism on earth: eat or be eaten. But as Jonah and Schweitzer discovered, there is a way out—the way of compassion for every living being.

᛬

Jonah seldom paid attention to the pagans or their stories. He'd encountered them often enough on his maritime travels— men of Byblos and Crete, Dalmatians and Ephesians—a regular Babel of tongues could be heard on shipboard, in Tarshish and other ports of call, each with their own gods and demi-gods and outlandish legends. Tales of mermaids and one-eyed monsters, flowers of forgetfulness and whirlpools that could suck you to the depths of Sheol were all too common. Sailors are a credulous lot, he'd noticed.

Besides, they were heathens. Most regarded Jonah as an oddity and some obviously resented the fact that he considered their beliefs mere superstitions. But they were the queer ones, Jonah told himself. They were the ones who prayed to idols! When not outright impiety, their yarns were simply nonsense.

But despite himself, Jonah did listen, and there was one he had heard quite often. A boy in the town of Hippo had been swimming one day when caught in the grip of an offshore current. A dolphin had pushed him back to land. The following day the dolphin returned, this time with a companion, and the boy and his friends watched as the animals played tag with the fishing boats, leaping in the surf. Overcoming their fears, the youngsters joined the animals in their antics and soon formed such a bond of trust that the children were riding on the dolphin's backs to school each day across the bay. Report of the marvel spread far and wide, so that the town began to attract visitors eager to see such a wonder, and Jonah himself had met a Cretan who claimed to have witnessed it. But then it was common knowledge that all Cretans were liars.

Jonah put such tall tales in the same category as the fable of Dionysos (as the Greeks called their god of wine.) According to the sailor's stories, Dionysos traveled from island to island, along with the entourage of wild beasts who almost always accompanied him, teaching men how to enjoy the fruit of the vine. One day, as he slept alone on a beach, a pirate ship sailed by. When they spied the richly clad youth, the pirates seized him, supposing they had kidnapped a wealthy prince for ransom. But when the god awoke, his fury was awful. Desperate to escape, the pirates threw themselves into the water. But they did not drown, for Dionysos took pity on them. He changed the sailors into dolphins, and that (said the Greeks) was why dolphins were the most human of all the creatures who lived in the sea.

Comparing people to overgrown sardines? Gods consorting with animals? That was sacrilege! Jonah had dismissed such legends out of hand.

Now the stories came back to him as he found himself holding tight to the dorsal fin of a large silver blue creature stronger and more graceful than any he had ever known. When he'd first felt the nudge in the middle of his back, Jonah had called loudly out to God, sure that he was going to be eaten. But instead of a shark, the Lord had sent him this— what he would have thought impossible before—a dolphin guiding him to shore.

That day Jonah had made three vows, as thanks for his rescue. Never again would he assume that knowledge of the Creator was limited to any Chosen People. Truth and falsehood, he realized, could be found among good people of every faith.

And never again, Jonah told himself, would he think of animals as anything less than beautiful or beloved in the eyes of God. Jonah had experienced a gentleness and intelligence he never would have guessed in the creature that became his savior.

Finally, Jonah vowed to tell his story and write it down, to bring others to an understanding of the One who is All Compassion. But who would believe it—riding ashore aback a great fish—the waterlogged prophet asked himself? Perhaps he might change one or two details in the telling, to make the whole thing easier to swallow.

Epilogue
Paradise Lost and Found

T HE AUTHORS OF THE BIBLE LIVED IN A WORLD
extravagantly furnished with animals, species that have
now mostly disappeared. Gazelles and wild goats were
common in the hills of Canaan, and the book of Judges expresses
no astonishment that Samson came upon a lion among the
vineyards of Judah. Job discloses that crocodiles wallowed in the
waters of the Jordan. Tigers could still be found in northern Persia
and Mesopotamia up until the early centuries of the Christian era.
But even before the Jews went down into Egypt, elephants,
rhinoceroses, and giraffes had mostly vanished from the Nile
Valley. And two hundred years before Jesus was born, leopards had
been eradicated from their range in Asia Minor, while wolves and
jackals were limited to the remote mountains. Now the only place
you might see lions or gazelles in Israel is at the 250-acre Safari
Park in Tel Aviv, from an enclosed tramway.

The Fertile Crescent, which Genesis identifies as the location of the original Garden of Eden, really was a paradise at one time, or at least amazingly lush. As Evan Eisenberg describes the region in *The Ecology of Eden*:

> *Although there were still marshes in the south, and plenty of semidesert in which seminomads as well as villagers and cityfolk grazed their herds, a wide tract of land on either side of the Euphrates was generously spangled with grainfields, date plantations, fishponds, and gardens of lettuce, onions, lentils, garlic, and cress.*

Mesopotamia (the country currently called Iraq) became the breadbasket of the Middle East. The agricultural surplus was made possible by the annual flooding of the rivers and by an extensive system of canals, dikes, and levees, that trapped the waters during the spring run off and then delivered them to the parched land when and where moisture was needed.

But disaster was in the making. Deforested hills brought increasing silt into the flood plains, slowly raising the water table and bringing more brine to the surface of the ground, where high temperatures and rapid evaporation left a thick layer of salt. The only solution was to leave the land fallow and unirrigated, to let watertables fall. But this was politically and strategically impossible. As the seat of world power, Sumer depended on its harvests to feed its growing armies and expanding population.

The Biblical legend of the Tower of Babel preserves a memory of the debacle that followed. The ziggurat, a stepped pyramid of sun-fired brick, was the chief architectural ornament of Sumerian cities like Ur and Kish, the tallest man-made object of the time. Like skyscrapers in the modern city, the ziggurat demonstrated human mastery of the environment and our ability to marshal the resources of nature to achieve our own ends. But by 2000 BCE there were alarming reports in Sumer of "the earth turned white," distinct references to the increasing salinization of the soil. And within two centuries, the Sumerian Empire had expired. Paradise had vanished. We were expelled from the cradle of civilization, not by God but rather by our own hand, and not for partaking of forbidden fruit, but for pushing nature past its allowable limits. No cherubim with flaming swords were placed on watch to prevent our re-entering the Garden, for none were needed. The land had become a barren desert, incapable of supporting life, and it remains desolate to this day.

The Bible says the Tower of Babel was destroyed when people could no longer understand each other's speech. But perhaps the catastrophe took place because human beings had forgotten how to speak an even older and more primal language—because they could no longer communicate intuitively with the earth and her creatures. In either case, hubris was involved. People imagined they had godlike powers to shape the natural world in their own image. The question now is whether we can learn from the past. Will we merely repeat the stories that have been passed down, or revise them, to write our own religious history?

Surely the great Book of Life cannot already be drawing to a close, with so much still in store. But if our planet has a future, then the chapters that remain to be written must do more than reiterate tales of times gone by. There can be little doubt that our sacred literature is in need of renewal, born of the dawning ecological consciousness that all creatures are interrelated and that all life is sacred. Our new Bible must draw on many sources— the wisdom of native peoples, the spirituality of the East, and the insights of feminism, as well as from the unspoken but powerful teachings of our furred, feathered and finny kindred, who embody a balance and simplicity that humankind desperately needs if we are to avoid destroying Eden once again (perhaps for the very last time). The teachings we need, like our current scriptures, cannot be fashioned overnight, but will be years in the making and may always remain unfinished—a work in progress—so long as people continue to seek the saving knowledge of how to live in *shalom*, in peace and friendship with all beings, or at least until the lion lies down with the lamb.

Whether we are at the beginning or the end of the human saga will depend on what we do and say, the lives we lead and the values we pass on to the young, including the stories that we tell. It is written that "a little child shall lead them" and for me, it was my young son Noah who encouraged me to begin the process of re-examining our religious roots and revising our spiritual traditions. But the tales and commentaries I have collected here are more suggestive than definitive—hardly more than a start. I look forward with hope to the book that remains to be written: *The Bible According to Noah*.

Sources and Suggestions for Further Reading

Sources

Ascione, Frank R. "Children Who Are Cruel To Animals: A Review of Research and Implications for Developmental Psychopathology," **Anthrozoös**, v.6, n. 4, 1993.

Beltz, Walter. *God and the Gods: Myths of the Bible*, Penguin Books, New York, NY 1983.

Brown, Lester R., (ed.). *State of the World*, W.W. Norton & Company, New York, NY 2000

Brown, Stuart L. "Animals at Play," **National Geographic**, v. 186, n. 6, 1994.

Buttrick, George Arthur, (ed.). *The Interpreter's Dictionary of the Bible*, Abingdon Press, Nashville, TN 1962.

Carpenter, Clarence R. "Behavior and Social Relations of Free-Ranging Primates," **The Scientific Monthly**, v. 48, 1939.

———. "A field study in Siam of the behavior and social relations of the gibbon (Hylobates lar)," **Comparative Psychology Monographs**, v. 16, n. 5, 1940.

D'Aulaire, Ingri and Edgar. *Book of Greek Myths*, Bantam Doubleday Dell, New York, NY 1992.

Davis, Edward B. "A Whale of a Tale: Fundamentalist Fish Stories," **Perspectives on Science and Christian Faith**, v. 43, 1991.

Diamond, Louise. *The Courage for Peace: Daring To Create Harmony in Ourselves and the World*, Conari Press, Berkeley, CA 1999.

Eisenberg, Evan. *The Ecology of Eden*, Alfred A. Knopf, New York, NY 1998.

Felthous, Alan R. and Stephen R. Kellert. "Violence Against Animals and People: Is Aggression Against Living Creatures Generalized?" **Bulletin of the American Academy of Psychiatry and the Law**, v. 14, n. 1, 1986.

Fine, Aubrey H., (ed.). *Handbook on animal-assisted therapy: theoretical foundations and guidelines for practice*, Academic, San Diego and London, 2000.

Flynn, Clifton. "Exploring the Link Between Corporal Punishment and Children's Cruelty to Animals," **Journal of Marriage and the Family**, v. 6, 1999.

——. "Why Family Professionals Can No Longer Ignore Violence Toward Animals," **Family Relations**, v. 49, no. 1, 2000.

Francis, Sandra. "The Origins of Dance: The Perspective of Primate Evolution" **Dance Chronicle**, v. 13, n. 2–3, 1991.

Gillard, E. Thomas. *Birds of Paradise and Bower Birds*, Weidenfeld & Nicolson, London, 1969.

Goodall, Jane. *Reason for Hope: A Spiritual Journey*, Warner Books, New York, NY 1999.

Gulik, R.H. Van. *The Gibbon in China: An Essay in Chinese Animal Lore*, E.J. Brill, Leiden, Holland, 1967.

Heinrich, Bernd. *Ravens in Winter*, Summit Books, New York, NY 1989.

——. *A Year in the Maine Woods*, Addison-Wesley, Reading, MA 1994

Hellman, Daniel S. and Nathan Blackman. "Enuresis, Firesetting and Cruelty to Animals: A Triad Predictive of Adult Crime," **American Journal of Psychiatry**, v. 122, 1966.

Hoedeman, Paul. *Hitler or Hippocrates: Medical experiments and euthanasia in the Third Reich*, The Book Guild, Sussex, England, 1991.

Lauck, Joanne. *The Voice of the Infinite in the Small: Revisioning the Insect-Human Connection*, Swan Raven & Co., Mill Spring, NC 1998.

Levenson, Jon D. *The Death and Resurrection of the Beloved Son: The Transformation of Child Sacrifice in Judaism and Christianity*, Yale University Press, New Haven and London, 1993.

Levinson, Boris. *Pets and Human Development*, Thomas, Springfield, IL 1972.

Lifton, Robert J. *The Nazi Doctors: Medical Killing and the Psychology of Genocide*, Basic Books, New York, NY 1986.

Lockwood, Randall. "The Tangled Web of Abuse: The Links between Cruelty to Animals and Human Violence," *The Humane Society News*, Summer 1986.

Lorenz, Konrad. *King Solomon's Ring*, Thomas Y. Crowell Company, New York, NY 1952.

Marshall, Joe T. and Elsie R. Marshall. "Gibbons and Their Territorial Songs," **Science**, n. 4249, 1976.

Masserman, Jules, Stanley Wechkind, and William Terris. "Altruistic Behavior in Rhesus Monkeys," **American Journal of Psychiatry**, v. 121, 1964.

Messadié, Gerald. *A History of the Devil*, Kodansha International, distributed by Farrar, Straus & Giroux, New York, NY 1996.

Milgram, Stanley. *Obedience to Authority: An Experimental View*, Harper & Row, New York, NY 1974.

Moscati, Sabatino. *The Face of the Ancient Near East: A Panorama of Near Eastern Civilizations in Pre-Classical Times*, Anchor Books, Garden City, NY 1960.

Osman, Major W. H. *Pigeons in World War II: The Official Records of the Performances of Racing Pigeons with the Armed Forces*, The Racing Pigeon Publishing Co., Ltd., London 1950.

Pagels, Elaine. *The Origin of Satan*, Random House, New York, NY 1995

Patterson, Gareth. *My Soul Amongst Lions*, St. Martin's Press, New York, NY 1996.

Payne, Roger. *Among Whales*, MacMillan, New York, NY 1993.

Ponting, Clive. *A Green History of the World: The Environment and the Collapse of Great Civilizations*, St. Martin's Press, New York, NY 1991.

Roberts, Elizabeth and Elias Amidon (eds.). *Earth Prayers*, HarperSanFrancisco, New York, NY 1991.

Ryden, Hope. *God's Dog: A Celebration of the North American Coyote*, Viking Press, New York, NY 1975.

Sagan, Carl and Ann Druyan. *Shadows of Forgotten Ancestors*, Random House, New York, NY 1992.

Schweitzer, Albert. *The Teaching of Reverence for Life*, Holt, Reinhart and Winston, New York, NY, 1965.

Sheridan, Charles and Richard King, Jr. "Obedience to Authority with An Authentic Victim," **Proceedings of the American Psychological Association**, v. 80, 1972.

Skutch, Alexander. *Life of the Pigeon*, Cornell University Press, Ithaca and London 1991.

Small, Meredith F. "Aping Culture," **Discover**, v. 21, n. 5, 2000.

Sparks, John. *The Discovery of Animal Behavior*, Little, Brown & Company, Boston and Toronto, 1982.

Strauss, Walter L. *The German Single-Leaf Woodcut 1550-1600: A Pictorial Catalogue*, Abaris Books, Inc., New York, NY 1975.

Swindler, D. R. (ed.). *Comparative Primate Biology*, Alan R. Liss, New York, NY 1986.

Watts, Alan. *Myth and Ritual in Christianity*, Beacon Press, Boston, MA 1968.

Wills, Garry. *Papal Sin: Structures of Deceit*, Doubleday, New York, NY 2000.

Wilson, Alexander. "The Wild Pigeon," in Hal Borland (ed.), *Our Natural World*, Doubleday & Company, Garden City, NY 1965

Suggestions for Further Reading

Berry, Thomas. *The Dream of the Earth*, Sierra Club Books, San Francisco, CA 1990.

Birch, Charles and John B. Cobb, Jr. *The Liberation of Life: From the Cell to the Community*, Cambridge University Press, New York, NY 1981.

Bradley, Ian. *God Is Green: Ecology for Christians*, Doubleday, New York, NY 1992.

Hyland, J. R. *God's Covenant With Animals*, Lantern Books, New York, NY 2000.

Kowalski, Gary. *The Souls of Animals*, Stillpoint Publishing, Walpole, NH 1991, Revised Edition 1999.

Linzey, Andrew. *Animal Gospel*. Westminster John Knox, Louisville , KY 1999.

———. *Christianity and the Rights of Animals*, Crossroad, New York, NY 1989.

———. *Animal Theology*. Illinois University Press, Urbana, IL 1995.

———. and Dorothy Yamamoto (eds.) *Animals on the Agenda.* Illinois University Press, Urbana, IL 1998.

Morris, Richard Knowles and Michael W. Fox (eds.). *On the Fifth Day: Animal Rights and Human Ethics*, Acropolis Books LTD, Washington, D.C. 1978.

Randour, Mary Lou. *Animal Grace: Entering a Spiritual Relationship with our Fellow Creatures*, New World Library, Novato, CA 2000.

McDaniel, Jay. *Of God and Pelicans: A Theology of Reverence for Life.* Westminster John Knox, Louisville, KY 1989.

Murti, Vasu. *They Shall Not Hurt or Destroy: Animal Rights and Vegetarianism in the Western Religious Traditions.* Available from 30 Villanova Lane, Oakland, CA 94611, 1995. Also www.jesusveg.com

Pinches, Charles, and Jay McDaniel eds. *Good News for Animals?: Christian Approaches to Animal Well-Being.* Orbis, Maryknoll, NY 1993.

Regan, Tom (ed.). *Animal Sacrifices: Religious Perspectives on the Use of Animals in Science,* Temple University Press, Philadelphia, PA 1986.

Regenstein, Lewis. *Replenish the Earth,* Crossroad, New York, NY 1991.

Rosen, Steven. *Diet for Transcendence: Vegetarianism and the World Religions,* Torchlight, Badger, CA 1996.

Ruether, Rosemary Radford. *Gaia and God: An Ecofeminist Theology of Earth Healing,* HarperCollins, New York, NY 1992

Schwartz, Richard. *Judaism and Vegetarianism.* Lantern Books, New York 2001.

Schweitzer, Albert. *Out of My Life and Thought,* New American Library, New York, NY 1953.

Singer, Peter. *Animal Liberation: A New Ethic for our Treatment of Animals,* Avon Books, New York, NY 1975.

Tobias, Michael and Kate Solisti-Mattelon (eds.). *Kinship with the Animals,* Beyond Words Publishing, Hillsboro, OR 1998.

Webb, Stephen H. *On God and Dogs: A Christian Theology of Compassion for Animals.* Oxford University Press, New York, 1997.

Young, Richard Alan. *Is God a Vegetarian? Christianity, Vegetarianism, and Animal Rights.* Open Court Publishing, Chicago IL 1999.